Towns
of
Nova Scotia

Rankings and Profiles

Richard Rogers

FOUR
EAST
PUBLICATIONS

Editing by Bronwen Hook
Layout and design by Richard Rogers
Cover layout and design by Brenda Conroy
Maps by Paul McCormick
Author photo by Bev Lamb
Front cover photo was taken by the author during a trip to Windsor in 2002.
Back cover includes the following photos by the author: The Wrestlers, a trademark of Stanfield's underwear products in the early years of the company; An historic Lunenburg home; The Heritage Museum in Antigonish; A view of Yarmouth's waterfront and Baintons in Annapolis Royal.

Published by Four East Publications
P.O. Box 3087, Tantallon, Nova Scotia B3Z 4G9

Distributed by Glen Margaret Publishing
www.glenmargaret.com

1st printing May 2006

Printed in Canada

Library and Archives Canada Cataloguing in Publication

Rogers, Richard, 1944-
    Towns of Nova Scotia / Richard Rogers.

Includes bibliographical references.
ISBN 0-920427-72-3

    1. Cities and towns—Nova Scotia—Guidebooks.
2. Nova Scotia—Guidebooks. I. Title.

FC2306.R63 2006   917.1604'5   C2005-906018-2

To Grayce
Blake and Owen

Sources

Place-Names and Places of Nova Scotia, facsimile edition printed by Mika Publishing Company, Belleville, Ontario, 1974, ISBN 0-919302-90-4, originally published by the Public Archives of Nova Scotia, Halifax, NS. This title was used extensively for the place names and history sections of this book. The other title that was helpful for these sections was *The Macmillan Book of Canadian Place Names* by William B. Hamilton, The Macmillan Company of Canada Ltd., 1978, ISBN 0-7705-1524-X.

The information for most of the the ratings was derived from the 2001 Census, available on the Statistics Canada website under 2001 Community Profiles:
www12.statcan.ca/English/Profil01/CP01 index.cfm?Lang=E

The rankings for area in square kilometres and date of incorporation were based upon information from the Annual Report of Municipal Statistics for the fiscal year ended March 31, 2002, ISSN 0383-4840, published in 2004 by Service Nova Scotia and Municipal Relations. The ranking of plant hardiness zones was based on information from Agriculture and Agri-Food Canada, plant hardiness zones of Canada 2000:
sis.agr.gc.ca/cansis/nsdb/climate/hardiness/intro.html

Photo credits

The photos of the Town Hall on page 12 and Pumpkin Welcome on page 15 were supplied by the Town of Kentville.

The photos of the Strait of Canso Yacht Club on page 16 and Granville Green on page 19 were supplied by the Town of Port Hawkesbury.

The photos of Samson Trail on page 28 and Welcome Sign on page 31 were supplied by the Town of New Glasgow.

The photos of River Phillip and the Wild Blueberry and Maple Centre on page 75 were both taken by Amy McCormack and supplied by the Town of Oxford.

The photo of Stanfest on page 108 was taken by Alan and Pam Samson and supplied by the Town of Canso.

Kentville's pumpkin people

Acknowledgements

I could not have written this book without the co-operation of many knowledgeable town officials who generously gave me the information that I needed. My thanks go to Roger MacIsaac, Amherst; Sharon McAuley (2005) and Ken Maher (2006), Annapolis Royal; Brian MacNeil and Mayor Kathleen Chisholm, Antigonish; Linda Parker (2002) and Carol Boylan (2005), Berwick; Sandra V. Bennett and Steve Raftery, Bridgetown; Carol Pickings-Anthony and Ken Smith, Bridgewater; Bill MacMillan and Mayor Ray White, Canso; Brian Crowell, Clark's Harbour; Linda Fraser (2002) and Tom Ossinger (2005), Digby; Jeff Lawrence, Hantsport; Carol Harmes and Bill Boyd, Kentville; Joyce Young, Lockeport; Bea Renton, Lunenburg; Kyle Hiltz (2002) and Jim Wentzell (2005), Mahone Bay; Raymond C. Rice, Middleton; Sam Murray (2002) and Roy Germon (2005) Mulgrave; Kimberly K. Dickson, New Glasgow; Darrell White and Crystal Rushton, Oxford; Ashley Brown, Parrsboro; David L. Steele and Jodie Noiles, Pictou; Colin J. MacDonald and Paula Davis, Port Hawkesbury; Mayor P.G. Comeau, Shelburne; Guy Brown and Donald F. Tabor, Springhill; B.V. (Van) MacLeod, Stellarton; Sheldon Dorey and Dallas, Stewiacke; Debbie Kampen, Trenton; James K. Langille and Juanita Bigelow, Truro; B.V. (Van) MacLeod, Westville; VanEssa Roberts, Windsor; J. Roy Brideau and Andrew Fry, Wolfville; and David Warner, Yarmouth.

Town of Canso from wharf

The Author

Richard Rogers came to Halifax, Nova Scotia, from New England in 1966 and worked as a teacher. After a few months in Montreal during Expo '67, he moved to Saskatchewan and taught in the small prairie community of Dinsmore. He returned to Halifax and graduated from Dalhousie University with a theatre degree in 1970. Married in the same year to a girl from Cape Breton, they traveled to Victoria, B.C., where he studied creative dramatics with children at the University of Victoria. They returned to Nova Scotia in 1971 and, after living briefly in Bridgewater, moved to Halifax, where he used his teaching and dramatic skills in the child life department of the IWK.

Richard started his career in book publishing in 1972, when he represented McGraw-Hill Ryerson as their educational representative in the Atlantic Provinces. In 1973 he and his wife moved to Seabright, a small community on St. Margaret's Bay near Peggy's Cove, where they remained until 1998,

when they moved to the nearby community of Glen Margaret, by then part of the HRM. His career in book publishing would include acting as the Atlantic representative for national and international companies such as Oxford University Press, the University of Toronto Press, MacMillan Canada and McClelland and Stewart. He served as the Atlantic representative for Penguin Books Canada from 1980 until 1997. During his career in publishing he has traveled extensively throughout Nova Scotia and the three other Atlantic Provinces.

From 1977 until 1985, Richard worked as an independent commission agent, which allowed him to represent several companies at the same time. He was the first to offer sales representation to the regional publishers and, as a result, represented Petheric (based in Halifax), Formac (based in Antigonish), Brunswick (based in Fredericton) and Lancelot (based in Hantsport). As regional publishing became a special interest, he created his own publishing company, Four East Publications, which has published over sixty titles dealing with Atlantic Canada. This is the first Four East book written by the publisher.

Introduction

Although there are many excellent communities in Nova Scotia, this book concerns itself with Nova Scotia's 31 incorporated towns, which, with the exception of Port Hawkesbury, are spread across the mainland of Nova Scotia. The other Cape Breton towns, and some mainland towns, lost their town status in the forced amalgamations of the 1990s. The incorporated towns vary dramatically, with the population of Truro, the largest, being 11,457 (2001), and Annapolis Royal, the smallest, being only 550 (2001). However, population size is not a qualification for town status, as some of Nova Scotia's villages have populations larger than Annapolis Royal.

The towns have been ranked based on 14 diverse criteria, which test strengths in a number of areas. While it is unlikely that any individual would use all of these criteria to choose their ideal town, the criteria can easily be personalized. You need only choose the criteria that are important to you, and, by doing the math, you can determine your top towns. You might ask if it was fair to compare towns that differ so dramatically in size, but the results do not favour the larger towns. In fact, the top three towns are of medium size.

Having visited all of the towns and taken nearly all of the pictures, I know far more about the towns than I could convey in the pages of this book. Additional and updated information can be found on our website: glenmargaret.com (click on towns). I would also encourage you to visit your favourites in order to better understand what they have to offer. All of them are on or near the sea and the most remote is only four hours from the Halifax

Regional Municipality. All have lower crime rates than urban areas and are especially welcoming to young families and new businesses. The Annapolis Valley towns are linked by Kings Transit, which is enjoying increasing ridership and buying new buses. At present, real estate in most of the towns of Nova Scotia is affordable, but prices will increase as they grow in popularity.

The Atlantic region has resisted the North American trend of moving to urban centres and is alone on the continent in retaining a balance similar to that found in the middle of the 20th century. Nova Scotia's towns can take some credit for this as they remain attractive places to live and work.

While extolling their virtues, I would be remise if I did not also include a few concerns. Some towns have had excessive levels of trihalomethane (THM, a suspected cancer-causing agent), in their water supplies. THM is formed when organic matter such as leaves mixes with chlorine in municipal water systems. Several towns have switched to using wells for their water supply to deal with the problem, and it should be noted that most towns that draw their water from surface sources do not exceed the national standard.

Another concern is the serious doctor shortage in Nova Scotia. It would be wise to determine that you will have access to a family doctor in any town that you are considering, especially if your health is compromised in any way. In addition, if you currently have a breathing disorder, you should be aware that the summer heat can form smog from pollutants moving into Nova Scotia from the industrial heartland of the continent.

Energy related concerns include liquefied natural gas plants (LNG). These plants have been rejected by many communities in the USA as they have the potential of creating an explosion that would affect a 5–10 mile radius. Point Lepreau, a nuclear power plant located near Saint John, creates a potential for destruction over a much greater area, and the Province of New Brunswick recently decided to refurbish and expand the plant, rather than decommission it. Finally, the Nova Scotia Power Corporation seems to be convinced that coal is the best fuel for Nova Scotia electrical generation, despite the pollution it creates.

As for the future, consider this. Dr. Roy Bishop wrote on the Valley web that at mid-tide, the flow of the Minas Channel north of Blomidon equals the combined flow of all the rivers and streams on earth! As 14 billion tonnes (14 cubic kilometres) of sea water flows into the Minas Basin twice daily, Nova Scotia actually bends and the countryside tilts slightly under the immense load. The highest tides on planet earth occur near Wolfville, in Nova Scotia's Minas Basin. All of this convinces me that Nova Scotia will be a major exporter of energy in the future and it will not be based on coal. Currently we are seeing developments in renewable wind and geothermal energy production, and with new technology now being developed, our massive tidal power potential will be exploited to the advantage of Nova Scotians living throughout the province.

View of the Town of Parrsboro

The Towns

Key to overall rankings

A = land base
B = early town status
C = affordable housing
D = full-time earnings
E = family income
F = employment rate
G = climate for gardening
H = university educated
I = multicultural population
J = number of children
K = growth over 5 years
L = growth over 40 years
M = population density
N = single population

Please note: The descriptions of the rankings are abbreviated for clarity. For a full description, see the individual charts at the back of this book. You should also note that towns with the same rankings indicate tied scores.

		a	b	c	d	e	f	g	h	i	j	k	l	m	n	
1	Kentville	4	5	26	10	4	9	19	3	7	20	6	6	14	7	140
2	Port Hawkesbury	16	7	19	4	3	4	19	14	22	4	17	1	19	3	152
3	Antigonish	23	7	27	5	2	17	8	2	5	19	13	7	30	1	166
4	Pictou	17	1	6	6	8	7	8	13	18	11	20	24	21	15	175
5	New Glasgow	12	2	17	2	7	18	8	10	11	20	22	11	31	10	181
6	Wolfville	19	16	30	3	1	10	19	1	1	27	26	4	25	2	184
7	Truro	1	2	21	19	22	18	8	5	11	26	23	13	11	5	185
8	Stellarton	15	7	10	8	10	16	8	14	22	7	19	17	22	15	190
9	Windsor	13	4	24	17	21	14	19	11	11	18	4	10	18	7	191
10	Stewiacke	3	23	20	9	19	22	19	25	11	1	9	5	2	24	192
11	Westville	6	17	5	16	24	23	8	27	22	2	14	12	8	10	194
12	Mulgrave	2	30	7	11	27	3	8	29	29	3	7	28	1	10	195
12	Shelburne	14	24	11	12	18	1	1	20	11	15	29	26	6	7	195
14	Bridgewater	7	20	25	14	12	11	19	12	7	23	3	3	23	20	199
15	Berwick	18	30	23	7	11	12	19	8	18	10	2	2	16	24	200
16	Oxford	10	22	9	26	17	8	19	16	22	12	11	16	4	24	216
16	Lunenburg	24	6	28	1	13	21	1	4	7	27	9	25	26	24	216
18	Amherst	8	7	13	24	26	5	8	19	22	14	12	20	29	15	222
19	Clark's Harbour	28	28	15	31	5	2	1	29	18	5	20	8	15	18	223
19	Yarmouth	11	13	18	22	31	24	1	18	18	6	8	21	28	4	223
21	Bridgetown	25	19	12	21	16	27	19	17	3	17	1	9	9	29	224
22	Hantsport	30	18	22	15	6	13	19	7	11	8	23	22	22	31	247
23	Springhill	9	7	2	20	25	30	8	26	29	22	14	29	17	10	248
24	Middleton	21	26	16	18	14	31	19	20	4	16	18	14	13	21	251
25	Canso	22	21	1	29	15	6	19	22	31	25	31	23	5	5	255
25	Trenton	20	27	4	23	23	15	8	28	22	9	27	19	20	10	255
27	Parrsboro	5	7	8	30	30	29	8	24	22	13	28	27	3	22	256
28	Annapolis Royal	31	15	31	13	20	20	1	8	1	30	30	30	7	22	259
29	Digby	26	13	14	28	28	25	1	23	7	29	23	14	27	18	276
30	Lockeport	29	24	3	27	29	28	1	31	11	24	5	31	10	24	277
31	Mahone Bay	27	28	29	25	9	26	19	6	6	31	16	18	12	30	282

Overall ranking of towns

Source: Based on Statistics Canada Census 2001 Community Profiles

Clockwise: Cornwallis Inn, Bed and Breakfast on a summer day, and Town Hall

1

Kentville

Original Names

Mi'kmaq name: Penooek (Pineo's Place)
French: Les Mines, an Acadian village, may have included the site of the town
English: Kentville, changed from Horton Corner in 1826, to honour the Duke of Kent

History

By 1800 the village of Horton Corner was comprised of fourteen houses and Henry Magee's store. Across the Cornwallis River, Negro settlements were created after the War of 1812, which had resulted in many former slaves fleeing to Canada as refugees. A central school for Kings County was built in the newly renamed Kentville in 1826-1827, and a post office was established in 1828.

The railway was completed to Kentville in August 1868, while the Central Valley Railway Company, with lines between Kentville and Kingsport, was opened in 1890 and sold to the D.A.R. in 1892.

The area surrounding the town contains some of the richest farmland in Nova Scotia. An agricultural society was founded as early as 1789, while a farm for an Experimental Horticultural Station was started in 1911. In 1959, its name was changed to the Kentville Regional Research Station. Canada Foods Limited was established in 1943, and the A.C.A. Co-Operative Association was founded in 1945.

Due to the importance of the local apple orchards, the annual Apple Blossom Festival was launched in Kentville in 1933. It has grown to include events throughout the entire Annapolis Valley.

Kentville today

Kentville is known as the "shire town of Kings County" and also as "the business and service center of the Valley". It benefits from the retail strength of adjacent New Minas, and the educational excellence of Acadia University in neighboring Wolfville. As the largest town in the Valley, Kentville is home to many government facilities, as well as legal, financial and medical services. While being within commuting distance of Halifax, it offers the lifestyle of a Valley town and many of the amenities of the city.

Employment is well diversified with the agri-food sector being prominent. The Kentville Agricultural Centre (previously known as the Agricultural Research Station) is one of the largest employers. As one of the most modern research facilities in Canada, it serves the Valley's important apple industry.

The largest non-agricultural employer for the region is Michelin Tire, located in nearby Waterville. A $92 million expansion in 2006/7 will make it the second largest truck-tire plant in the worldwide Michelin group. The expansion will enable it to produce the double-width X-One truck tires that have been shown to save up to 10 per cent in fuel costs and reduce greenhouse gas emissions.

A new water treatment system, completed in 2002, provides well water from an underground aquifer found at the west end of town. The two enclosed glass-lined steel reservoirs solved quality problems, especially the high THM levels of the previous system that used lake water. The additional quantity of water provided by the new system has allowed for the opening of new residential lots. A sophisticated sewage treatment plant serves the needs of Kentville's residents and discharges into the Cornwallis River.

Kings County Academy offers elementary grades within the town, while other grades are bused to nearby regional facilities. Kentville's community college, Kingstec, recently received a $13 million upgrade as part of a provincial initiative to invest in the community college network. This has resulted in increased capacity for 469 students and additional programs. Kentville is also the home of Valley Regional Hospital, which provides the highest level of care available outside Halifax. Kings Transit connects Kentville to other Valley towns.

Kentville offers an array of recreational and sports facilities, even an indoor facility for soccer. Volunteerism is strong and the town hosts many activities. In the spring, the Apple Blossom Festival is a major attraction and in the fall, the Annual Harvest Festival attracts many visitors who marvel at the world famous Pumpkin People.

The town has shown leadership by acquiring a centrally-located eight-hectare parcel of land that was owned by the CPR. Working with a local developer, the first phase will see an assisted living complex, known as Kings Riverside Court, provide 45 apartments for seniors in 2006. The later two phases will house services for seniors and residential care units. This is seen as the centerpiece of Kentville's future, ensuring the town a healthy mix of residential and commercial services.

Kentville has been noted as having the highest per capita ratio of professionals in Canada. In addition, it has more sunny days each year than almost any other Nova Scotia community. Perhaps it is not surprising that this exceptional town was also able to pass a cat bylaw with no opposition.

Why 1st

Kentville finished 10th or better in 10 of the 14 categories. A 3rd place in university educated population was the strongest result, while a 4th in both land base and family income and a 5th for early town status also helped the overall placement. A 6th place in both population change categories (growth over 5 years and growth over 40 years), a 7th place for both multicultural population, and single population, all combined to give Kentville the best overall score.

I should also say that there were two weak placements, which included a 26th in affordable housing and a 20th in number of children. While they remain a concern, they were not enough to change the overall 1st place standing of this exceptional town.

Sources

www.town.kentville.ns.ca
www.michelin.com
www.nscc.ca/about_nscc/Locations Kingstec.asp
www.Kingsced.ns.ca pdfBriefsKCEDABriefsSep62005.pdf
www.kingstransit.ns.ca

Clockwise from top: Pumpkin Welcome, Valley Regional Hospital, the Nova Scotia Community College, Kentville Agricultural Centre sign, and bus depot.

Clockwise from top: Port Hawkesbury Civic Centre, Strait of Canso Yacht Club and Interior view of Port Hawkesbury Civic Centre.

2

Port Hawkesbury

Original Names

English: Port Hawkesbury, changed from an earlier name, Ship Harbour, in 1860 by an act of the legislature and believed to honour Charles Jenkinson, Baron Hawkesbury

History

The town plot of Hawkesbury was laid out on the north side of Ship Harbour late in the eighteenth century. Lieutenant-Governor Macarmick referred to Hawkesbury in 1790. A Methodist Church was built in 1828. There was a postal way office at Ship Harbour in 1829. James Newton and John MacKay were teaching 68 children in Ship Harbour by 1847. Ship Harbour became Port Hawkesbury in 1860.

As early as 1833, Ship Harbour (Port Hawkesbury) was a terminus of a Strait of Canso ferry service. In the 1860s a steam ferry was provided. By the end of the 1880s the Eastern Extension Railway was running from New Glasgow to the Strait of Canso. Subsequently, the Government of Canada purchased the Eastern Extension Railway and the Strait of Canso ferry steamer, the *S.S. Norwegian*,

which had been running between Wylde's Wharf and Grant's Wharf, Port Hawkesbury. In 1891 railway communication was established between Halifax and Sydney. In 1893 a new ferry steamer of steel, with two barges for carrying passenger and freight cars, was provided at the Strait of Canso.

The Canso Causeway was completed in 1955 from Auld's Cove to Port Hastings, which ended the ferry service.

The construction of a large pulp mill at nearby Point Tupper in 1960 caused a boom at Port Hawkesbury. A large shopping centre was built and housing development took place. The causeway also served to draw new business to Port Hawkesbury.

Port Hawkesbury Today

Port Hawkesbury is considered to be the home of Stora Enso, but this industrial giant is actually located in Point Tupper (Richmond County), one kilometer from Port Hawkesbury. The town is the centre of an industrial region that is attractive due to the Strait of Canso, the deepest harbour in the world, ice free and large enough for a super tanker to come in and out without difficulty. This is not an industrial town, although many residents work in nearby industry. It can more accurately be described as "the commercial and professional centre of the Strait area".

The Strait Area Gas Corporation, a consortium of the towns of Port Hawkesbury and Mulgrave and Rock Creek Energy, recently received regulatory approval to distribute natural gas to Antigonish, Inverness, Richmond and Guysborough counties. It is expected that as this new energy option develops it will attract new industries. This fits well in the overall energy strategy for the Strait region that will include a $450 million L.N.G. plant that is under construction near Point Tupper and expected to be operational by 2007.

Port Hawkesbury's water treatment plant was built in 1970 and upgraded in 1999. It draws water from Landry Lake. In 1969, Port Hawkesbury became one of the first towns in the province to install a sewage treatment plant. It currently has primary treatment, while the effluent is discharged into the Strait of Canso. A new sewage treatment plant that will provide secondary treatment will be completed in 2006.

Tamarak Education Centre serves the needs of students from primary to grade eight, while grades nine to twelve attend the Strait Area Education and Recreation Centre. Both schools are located within the town. The Strait area campus of the Nova Scotia Community College is also in Port Hawkesbury, while a short drive will take you to highly-rated St. Francis Xavier University in Antigonish.

Port Hawkesbury's new $18 million Civic Centre was the first in North America to use engineered natural daylight to illuminate the ice surface. The special glass units, provided by a company based in Cape Breton, allow the rink lights to be off on any sunny day. This provides near-perfect lighting, results in substantial energy savings and, as there is less heat, harder ice and less work for the ice-making plant. The environmentally friendly complex also benefits from a geothermal heating and cooling system. In addition to the ice surface, it includes a 500-seat convention centre, quilt market, arts studio, walking track, fitness centre, and municipal offices. The facility hosted the Grand Slam of Curling, an international event, in 2005, and in 2006 has been listed as one of the top ten sports stadiums in the world.

To further make Port Hawkesbury an attractive place to live, town developers are investing in a $25 million complex that will include a 100-unit condominium complex and a suite-style hotel. Pedways will link the condominiums and hotel to businesses and the Civic Centre. This will increase the housing options and help those requiring entry level single family homes in the Strait area.

During the summer season, visitors and residents are attracted to the waterfront as boats arrive and depart from the yacht club, while on summer Sunday evenings, the Granville Green series of free outdoor concerts feature some of Atlantic Canada's best performing artists.

Why 2ⁿᵈ

Port Hawkesbury earned a 7th place or better in the majority of the categories and did reasonably well in the others. The overall rating was boosted by a 1st in growth over 40 years, a 3rd for both single population and family income, and 4th in full-time earnings, employment rate and, very importantly, number of children.

Sources

www.townofporthawkesbury.ca
www.phcivic.com

Clockwise from top: Granville Green, Stora Enso, Town across water, Shopping centre and The Creamery on the waterfront.

Clockwise: Town Hall, The Dancer (a tree sculpture) and Court House.

3

Antigonish

Original Names

Mi'kmaq: Nalegitkoonechk (where branches are torn off)
French: Antigonish, derived from the Mi'kmaq name and known by this spelling as early as 1755
English name: Antigonish, 1821, after an unsuccessful attempt to establish settlement nearby under the name of Dorchester

History

In 1784 Colonel Timothy Hierlihy and the other officers and men of the Nova Scotia Volunteers received a grant of twenty-one thousand six hundred acres on Antigonish Harbour. The early settlement was at the entrance of Antigonish Harbour at what is called Town Point. Some of the settlers discovered that the soil was more fertile at the head of the tide and so sold their land at the harbour and moved up the river. Others found that large trees grew on the intervale and on the hills and cut these to float down the streams to Antigonish Harbour. A settlement called Antigonish Intervale developed at the junction of the West and Wright's Rivers. Here Nathaniel Symonds opened a shop in 1804 and, about 1806, he began to manufacture potash from wood ashes of the trees being cleared along the intervale.

In 1804 the Presbyterians organized a congregation at the home of Nathaniel Symonds, where they met until a small church was erected on what became Church Street.

The first Roman Catholic chapel in the village was built in 1810. A post office was established in 1816 at "The Village", which, as early as 1821, was called Antigonish.

A telegraph office was opened in Antigonish by the Nova Scotia Electric Telegraph Company in 1852. The Eastern Extension Railway was opened for traffic from New Glasgow to Antigonish in 1879, and from Antigonish to the station at Crittenden's Creek in 1880.

St. Francis Xavier University was founded as a

college in 1853 in temporary quarters at Arichat, Richmond County, but two years later was transferred to Antigonish. An engineering school was established in 1899. Mount St. Bernard College for women was affiliated in 1894, and St. Martha's School of Nursing in 1926.

An extension department was established in 1929 for work in adult education in the farming and fishing communities of eastern Nova Scotia. This work has spread to other parts of the world through the work of the Coady International Institute. Xavier Junior College was established as an integral part of the University at Sydney in 1951, to serve the needs of industrial Cape Breton.

The Sisters of St. Martha was founded in 1900, and St. Martha's Hospital was opened in 1906. The Highland Society was established in 1861 by Dr. Alexander McDonald, pioneer physician of Antigonish County, with the first Highland Games being held in 1863.

By the mid 20th century a large percentage of those living in the town were employed by the university. The town had a newspaper, *The Casket*, a 10,000 watt radio station, C.J.F.X., and a television outlet CFXV-TV. The industrial and commercial life of Antigonish depended mainly upon the surrounding farm area with a dairy, bakeries, machine shop, woodworking factory, contracting firms, a quarry and monument works, shops, banks and service industries providing employment.

Antigonish Today

Antigonish is located on Nova Scotia's north shore, midway between Halifax and Sydney. It is known as "the Highland Heart of Nova Scotia", which is appropriate, as this is the home of the Highland Games, the oldest celebration of Scottish sport and dance in North America. As Catholics make up 82% of the population, the town is also sometimes referred to as "the Little Vatican".

This is the primary centre in northeastern Nova Scotia for retail, government, education and healthcare services. The two largest employers are St. Francis Xavier University and Saint Martha's Regional Hospital; while numerous small businesses, when combined, provide a significant share of the total employment.

Antigonish is building a new seven million dollar water treatment plant to replace the current system that is 30 years old. The sewage treatment system is approximately 35 years old, and was upgraded in 1995. It provides secondary and tertiary treatment and discharges into Antigonish Harbour. The town has the largest of Nova Scotia's six municipally owned and operated electric utilities, which enables it to subsidize the tax rate and to offer additional services to the community.

This is the home of St. Francis Xavier University, judged Canada's top primarily undergraduate university. The presence of the university makes possible the rich cultural life available to residents, and the fine accommodations and restaurants that enrich their social life. Evidence of this rich cultural life is seen in Theatre Antigonish, which is the result of co-operation between "town and gown", and in the carvings around the town that have been made from dying elm trees.

The Antigonish Movement, the local community development movement that evolved from the work of Rev. Dr. Moses Coady and Rev. Jimmy Tompkins in the 1920s, is still alive today in the work of the Coady International Institute. Located on the campus of St. Francis Xavier University, it draws students from around the world for its programs in adult education and self help.

This appears to be a town without a weakness,

yet its very existence is in question as I write this in early 2006. To increase its small land base, Antigonish applied to annex land from the neighbouring County, which, in turn, applied for the amalgamation of town and county. The Nova Scotia Utilities and Review Board decided in favour of amalgamation and a plebiscite was only put on hold due to the town applying to the court to question the authority of the URB. The town has only one third the population of the county, so a plebiscite would be decided largely by county residents. We can hope that Antigonish will find a solution to this dilemma and retain its status as one of the leading towns in Nova Scotia.

Why 3rd?

One might ask why Antigonish was not 1st, as it has so many obvious advantages, but it was brought down in the overall ratings by three categories that are all connected to its current problems. It placed 30th in population density, 27th in affordable housing and 23rd in land base.

On the positive side was a 1st in single population, 2nd in both family income and university educated population, 5th in both full-time earnings and multicultural population and 7th in both early town status and growth over 40 years.

Sources

www.townofantigonish.ca
www.stfx.ca
www.coady.stfx.ca

St. Francis Xavier University, Coady International Institute, Saint Martha's Regional Hospital, and The Piper (a tree sculpture).

Clockwise from top: Grohmann Knives, Pictou Advocate, The Hector.

4

Pictou

Original Names

Mi'kmaq: Piktook (an explosion of gas)
French: La riviere de Pictou, applied to the harbour
by Nicholas Denys in the 1660's
English: Pictou. The town was laid out in 1788
mostly by those who had been passengers on the
Hector, although attempts were made to change
the name, this remains one of the oldest place
names on the north shore of Nova Scotia

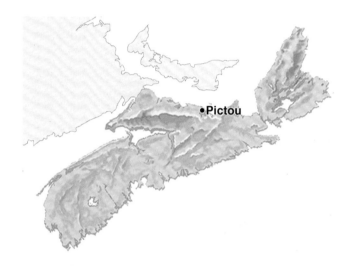

History

In 1763 a land grant was made to the Philadelphia
Company, whose first settlers (including Captain
Hull, Dr. John Harris, Robert Patterson, James
McCabe, John Rogers, and Henry Cumminger)
arrived from Pennsylvania on the brigantine *Betsey*
four years later. Then followed the first wave of
Highland Scots, on the *Hector*. This ship arrived
from Loch Broom, Scotland, in 1773 and the people
came ashore to found the town on land granted to
Alexander McNutt in 1765. The McNutt Grant was
escheated in 1770 and in August, 1783, part of it
was re-granted to forty-four people, mostly *Hector*
passengers. The arrival of the Loyalists in 1784
increased the population significantly. Pictou town
was laid out in 1788 and the first house was built in
1790.

A school was opened by Peter Grant about 1793.
A jail was built in 1792 and a courthouse was built
in 1813. Also in 1813, a post office was established.
In 1775 travel between Pictou and P.E.I. was by
birch bark canoe, but a regular packet was running
by 1825 and in 1830 the steam boat *Richard Smith*
was put on this route.

The original Pictou Academy building was
completed in 1818. A public subscription library
was established in 1822 and lasted about thirty
years. St. James Anglican Church was consecrated in
1829. A lighthouse was built at Cole Point in 1834.

The Pictou Railway between Pictou, Westville
and Stellarton was opened in 1887. A "Short Line"
between Oxford Junction and Pictou opened in
1890 and a new Intercolonial Railway Station and

roundhouse was built in 1905-1906.

Pictou's early industries were lumbering, fishing and shipbuilding. Hamilton's Bakery was established in 1840 and was purchased by Weston's Ltd. in 1955. Pictou Iron Foundry went into operation in 1856, and a coal-oil company was built in 1860. Robert Campbell operated a tannery in the 1860s and 1870s. The Pictou Gas Works were in operation in the 1870s and in 1871 the Pictou Boot and Shoe Company was incorporated. In 1906, Allan A. Ferguson purchased a foundry and developed the Pictou Foundry and Machine Company, changing its name to Ferguson Industries Limited in 1950 and primarily building steel ships since 1942. Other companies included Maritime Packers, that was acquired by National Sea Products in 1965; Pictou Cutlery Ltd., incorporated in 1949; Atlantic Milling Company Ltd.; Fred Magee Ltd., Canners; and Stright and MacKay, boat builders. In 1962, Pictou was a ship building refit and repair centre, a concentration and collection point for lobsters from the Northumberland Strait and salmon from Belle Isle Strait, and a major port for the export of lumber.

Pictou Today

Pictou is known as the birthplace of New Scotland and is today described as more Scottish than Scotland. Its history is the focal point of a growing tourism industry, along with the recent development of the waterfront. A replica of the tall ship Hector, which brought Pictou's original settlers from Scotland in 1773, is the centerpiece of this successful heritage development.

Pictou is known to most Nova Scotians as the home of a major paper manufacturer, but this plant, now known as Neenah Paper Inc., is actually in the county. Although it has improved in recent years, the town has contended with the negative environmental effects associated with the paper mill, while not enjoying the tax benefits. The paper is shipped from a pier in the town and this too has generated controversy, as innkeepers object to their patrons being disturbed by large trucks in the early morning hours.

Employers in the town include the internationally recognized Grohmann Knives Ltd., Advocate Printing and Publishing, and the retail and service sector, which is often tourism based. Although the shipyard is closed, there is some inshore fishing. Large regional employers include nearby Michelin Tire and Neenah Paper, as well as TrentonWorks Ltd.

Despite the consolidation of schools within Pictou County, Pictou has managed to retain its impressive high school, Pictou Academy. This enables students within the town to walk to school for all of their public schooling. The town lacks sewage treatment as this book is being published, but the design of a large sewage treatment facility has been completed, a site has been chosen, and the town is wisely working with the Municipality of Pictou County to include neighboring communities within the county. The town water system is old and is dependent upon fourteen wells that feed the system. It produces hard water, so considerable treatment is needed to remove minerals such as iron.

There is little room in the town to attract industry, so Pictou is apt to remain primarily residential and the home of small businesses. Its natural beauty will continue to attract tourists, as well as new and return residents who are seeking a higher quality of life.

Why 4th?

Pictou did very well in the ratings placing in the upper third in six categories. A 1st place for early town status, a 6th place in both affordable housing and full-time earnings, a 7th place for employment rate, and 8th place in both family income and climate for gardening all contributed to the excellent overall result.

The weakest results, and they were few, were a 24th place in growth over 40 years, a 21st place in population density, and a 20th place in growth over 5 years. Although the land base is considered a weakness, Pictou still placed a respectable 17th in this category.

Sources

www.townofpictou.com
www.neenahpaper.com
www.michelin.ca
www.grohmannknives.com
www.advocateprinting.com

Clockwise from top: Entrance sign, Pictou Academy, McCulloch House, The de Coste Centre and Stone building featuring a chimney window.

Clockwise from top: View of the bridge from the Samson Trail, Samson Trail and Marina, Town Hall on Provost Street.

5

New Glasgow

Original Names

English: New Glasgow, named after Glasgow, Scotland, by William Fraser, who first surveyed the townsite

History

Settlement by Scottish immigrants began in the 1780s and Alexander Fraser had built a mill here by 1793. A bridge was built across the East River near the head of the tide by 1803. Andrew Blair opened a school about 1812, and a school-house was built by 1818.

A Presbyterian church built on Frasers Mountain in 1819 was moved to New Glasgow in 1828 to form the beginnings of St. Andrew's congregation. A postal way office was established about 1834 and a post office was opened in 1841. A jail was built about 1838. The Intercolonial Railway was completed to New Glasgow from Truro by 1867. In 1886 a Y.M.C.A. building was opened and Aberdeen Hospital was constructed 1896-1897.

For a time in the mid-nineteenth century, the area prospered as a major shipbuilding centre. Prominent among the local shipbuilders was Captain George McKenzie (1798-1876), who became known as 'the father of shipbuilding in Pictou County'. His business flourished during the period when wooden vessels were needed for the timber trade with Great Britain and for the export of coal to the United States.

The Acadian Iron Foundry opened in 1867, and later became I. Matheson & Co. Maritime Steel and Foundries Ltd. was begun as a blacksmith shop in 1902. It amalgamated with the McPherson foundry in 1914. Standard Clay Products was founded by Wallace Trotter, Sr., in 1902. This plant was responsible for the growth of the suburb originally known as Pipetown and later called Parkdale. Steel Furnishing Co. Ltd. was founded in 1906 and incorporated in 1914. Cameron and Fraser Limited began in Pleasant Valley before 1905 and moved to New Glasgow in 1913, where they began making coffins in 1915. The New Glasgow Foundry was established in 1917 by Joseph Allan.

Eastern Woodworkers Limited was established by Harold Mingo in 1938. Gomac Construction Limited, a subsidiary, was formed in 1946. Tasco Sheet Metal and Roofing Co. began in 1955. L.E. Shaw Ltd. built a brick manufacturing plant in 1947 and a new plant in 1965. Other businesses at this time included Seven Up (New Glasgow) Ltd., McLeans Beverages Ltd., Acadian Coal Co. Ltd., Tidewater Construction, Imperial Oil Ltd., Farmers Co-op Dairy Ltd., Inter Supply Ltd., Canadian Oil Companies Ltd., Canadian Petrofina Ltd., and John J. Collie and Sons, Ltd.

New Glasgow Today

New Glasgow is the largest town in Pictou County, the second largest town in Nova Scotia and, when combined with adjacent towns, the third largest concentration of population in Nova Scotia. This is a commercial and service centre situated along the banks of the East River and known as "the Gateway to the River".

The retail sector is the largest source of employment within the town, but Convergys, a high tech customer service centre, is also providing an impressive number of jobs, while drawing business into the town. The industrial and service sectors are also significant, with Maritime Steel and the Pictou County Health Authority being the largest employers. Notable regional employers include Empire Company, Sobeys Inc., Neenah Paper Inc., TrentonWorks, Michelin and Scotsburn Dairy Co-op.

The town of New Glasgow has provided water to its residents for over 100 years, with the modern Forbes Water Treatment Facility opening in 2000. It draws water from Forbes Lake, which is located in the County. Designated a watershed by the province, it is owned and preserved by the town. In addition to supplying the needs of residents of New Glasgow, it also serves the town of Westville, parts of the County, as well as Nova Scotia Power and TrentonWorks. A sewage treatment system was created in the early 1970s and was upgraded in the 1990s. It is now called the East River Pollution Abatement Plant, serves the needs of the four towns and discharges into the East River.

All public school grades are available within the town from three elementary schools (A.G. Baillie Memorial, Acadia Street School, and Temperance Street School), a junior high school (New Glasgow Junior High), and a modern regional high school that opened in 2003 (North Nova Education Centre). The recently updated Nova Scotia Community College (Pictou Campus) is located in nearby Stellarton, while highly rated St. Francis Xavier University is within commuting distance in Antigonish.

This is the home of the Aberdeen Hospital, a regional hospital that serves Pictou County. The Pictou-Antigonish Regional Library has its headquarters here. Due to the strong community spirit and entrepreneurism, the town uses the phrase "built by enterprise – growing with imagination" to describe itself. It is also proud of its racial and gender diversity and promotes the fact that it is a multi-cultural mosaic.

Commercial and residential development peaked in 2004, setting a record for the town and reinforcing the importance of recent environmental and recreational improvements. Perhaps the next challenge facing New Glasgow is the revitalization of its downtown, without losing the architectural charm of its 19th century buildings.

The revitalized riverfront is a source of pride and has drawn many community gatherings and festivals to a riverside setting. Part of a larger trail system, the Samson Trail, a four kilometer trail created along the bed of Canada's first iron railroad, runs along the riverside and is heavily used by a variety of outdoor enthusiasts. The river flows into the nearby Northumberland Strait, which, in the past, allowed hundreds of ocean-going ships to be built here and, today, allows a full service marina to operate as part of New Glasgow's downtown.

Why 5th?

New Glasgow scored well in most categories and this balance resulted in 5th place overall. The most negative result was a 31st place in population density; while positive results included 2nd place in both early town status (only Pictou had a higher score in this category) and full-time earnings.

Sources

www.newglasgow.ca
www.parl.ns.ca
www.abdeenhospital.com

Clockwise from top: Welcome Sign, New Glasgow Library, Laurie Park and Shipbuilding Monument.

Clockwise from top: Acadia University, Gazebo at Waterfront Park and Blomidon Inn

6
Wolfville

Original Names

Mi'kmaq: Mtaban (mud-cat-fish ground)
English: Wolfville. Originally Mud Creek and then Upper Horton Post Office, it was changed to Wolfville in 1829 due to the prominence of the DeWolf family

History

There were some Acadian settlers in the area in the early 18th century, but in 1760 the Planters from New England arrived and settled the area known as Mud Creek. The earliest residents included Obediah Wickwire, James Woodman, Daniel DeWolf, Daniel Bigelow and Edward DeWolf.

St. John's Anglican Church was consecrated in 1826. A postal way office was established here about 1829, with Elisha DeWolf as postmaster. In 1867 a public school building was erected and a new Academy was built in 1874-1875.

Horton Academy, designed for the education of Baptist young men, was opened in 1829. The classes of Queens College began in the Academy building in 1839 and, in 1841, the name was changed to Acadia University with the granting of a charter.

A ladies seminary was opened in 1858 in a building that later became the Royal Hotel. It was known as the Grand Pre Seminary for ten years, with John Chase as headmaster. In 1879 it became known as the Acadia Seminary and occupied a new building built on the grounds of the university.

With the completion of a railway bridge over Mud Creek, the first train ran from Annapolis to Wolfville in 1869. Eastern Kings Memorial Hospital was opened in 1930, and the Randall House was restored and opened as a museum in 1949.

Kent Foods Limited established in Canning in 1946 and, in 1963, put a half-million dollar plant in Wolfville. In 1964, the Holland Bakery Limited closed after twenty-eight years in business. Retail has always been an important part of the economy.

Wolfville Today

Wolfville, a Valley town that looks upon Blomidon and the Minas Basin, is best known as the home of Acadia University. It uses the slogan "wonderful, welcoming" and its population doubles every September when the community "welcomes" new and returning Acadia students.

Wolfville is an academic centre with Wolfville School providing grades primary–9 within the town, while upper grades attend Horton High School, a modern regional high school in adjacent Greenwich. Landmark East, established in 1979, describes itself as Canada's leading international boarding and day school for students with learning difficulties. It accepts students from age 11-19. Fairfield School, established in 2002, is a democratic free school for ages 4-17. Acadia University, one of Canada's leading liberal arts universities, is also the town's largest employer.

The town benefits from its proximity to neighboring communities with complimentary services, especially the highly developed retail sector in nearby New Minas, and the business and government services available in Kentville, including the Valley Regional Hospital. Wolfville is also linked to other Valley towns through the regular bus service supplied by Kings Transit.

As this is one of Nova Scotia's most popular towns, it faces the challenge of accepting growth, while still protecting the quaint charm that attracts new residents. Some developments fit in well, including a condominium development called Railtown. It is being built on the waterfront at a site formerly occupied by a building supplies company. Demolition has proceeded slowly to maximize recycling and minimize waste going into the landfill. The 29 condos will be within walking distance of all of Wolfville's amenities.

Wolfville Harbour, the smallest registered port in North America, can be seen from Waterfront Park. The park also affords a view of the dykes built by the Acadians. The water treatment system that serves the town draws water from deep water wells, while the sewage treatment system provides primary treatment and discharges into the Minas Basin.

Wolfville welcomes over 65,000 spectators who take in cultural and sporting events at the Acadia Arena/Festival Theatre facilities each year. Other attractions include the centrally located Acadia Theatre: built in 1947, it has been restored by a co-op of local film and stage fans. It reopened as a 160 seat centre for cinema and live theatre. In addition, the Robie Tufts Nature Centre was built around a chimney that attracts hundreds of chimney swifts. Both tourists and locals are drawn to the site at dusk to see the birds enter the chimney for the night. The Centre is also home on Saturdays to a seasonal Farmers Market.

Wolfville has approximately 8 kilometres of trails within the town limits, making it one of the largest trail systems (per capita) in the province. It is the home of the K.C. Irving Centre, a multi-million dollar gift to Acadia University that includes the K.C. Irving Experimental Science Centre. This centre is dedicated to the study of the natural environment, concentrating on the ecology of the Acadian Forest Region (that includes Nova Scotia); and the Harriet Irving Botanical Gardens. The latter covers six acres, and contains 9 native habitats and a large collection of native plants, including rare and endangered species. Finally, visitors to Wolfville have access to perhaps the best collection of inns and fine dining in Nova Scotia, including the Blomidon Inn, Tattingtone, Victoria's Inn, Acton's and the Tempest.

Why 6th

Wolfville had four poor placements that prevented it from being the top town overall. The worst was 30th place in affordable housing, with 27th place for number of children, 26th place for growth over 5 years, and 25th place for population density also having a negative effect.

On the positive side, Wolfville placed 1st in three categories – family income, university educated population and multicultural population. Other placements that had a positive effect on the overall score included a 2nd for single population, 3rd for full-time earnings and 4th for growth over 40 years.

Sources

www.townwolfville.ns.ca
www.acadia.ca

Clockwise from top: Irving Centre at Acadia University, Willow Park, Harbour at low tide with Blomidon in distance, Robie Tufts Nature Centre and Clock on main street.

Clockwise from top: Bank of Nova Scotia Building – Inglis Place, Robert Stanfield (tree art), Entrance to Civic Building, Path in Victoria Park.

7

Truro

Original Names

Mi'kmaq: Wagobagitk (the bay runs far up or the
end of the waters flow)
French: Cobequid
English: Truro, for Truro, Cornwall, England

History

By 1720 there were about fifty French families at
Cobequid, or the Truro-Onslow area. In 1755 the
Acadians left this area to avoid deportation and
their villages were burned. In 1761, the transports
carrying people with the patronage of Colonel
Alexander McNutt arrived in the basin of Minas, and
the resettlement of Cobequid-Truro and Onslow
began. The new settlers were mainly Scots-Irish
from Ireland and from New Hampshire in New
England.

In 1768 the frame of a metting-house was
raised. This building was abandoned when the new
Presbyterian church was built about 1854 and in
1857 the frame was used in the construction of a
Temperance Hall.

A school was opened about 1775, near the
corner of Walker and Queen Streets. The Normal
School was established in 1855, which would become known as the Nova Scotia Teachers College by
1962. The Maritime Home for Delinquent Girls was
opened in 1914, and the Manual Training School in
1949.

A post office was established in 1812, and a post
office building was constructed before 1838. A
court-house and a jail were both erected in 1803. A
Fire Brigade was organized in 1868 and an engine
house was built around 1869. A new Town Hall was
completed in 1886. The Truro radio station, CKCL,
was established in 1947.

The Intercolonial Railway line from Halifax was
opened in 1858. The *Mirror and Colchester Adver-
tiser* was issued in 1867 by Isaac Baird.

The Truro Iron Foundry was established in 1862, and the Stanfields textile mills in 1868. By 1871, the industrial base also included the Truro Boot and Shoe Company, Lewis and Sons Sash and Peg Factory, two tanneries, and a railway car manufactory owned by Acadia Iron and Steel Company. The Truro Condensed Milk and Canning Company built a factory in 1883. The Brookfield Dairy Company moved to Truro in 1920.

Halliday Craftsmen Limited, makers of pre-fabricated homes began in Truro in 1928. By 1959, the major manufacturers included: Bordens Limited, Maritime Processing Limited, Dominion Tar and Chemical Company Limited, Halliday Craftsmen, Vibric Limited, Hawkins and Zwicker Limited, Eastern Felt Company, and Stanfields Limited. Godsell Equipment Limited, Mussins Limited, and Acadia Cordage Limited opened in 1963. Crossley-Karastan Carpet Mills and Abbey Wines both began production in 1965 and Electrical Distributors Limited opened the same year.

Truro has been known as a warehousing and distribution centre, with agriculture (especially dairy) and lumber production being the principal occupations in the surrounding area.

Truro Today

Truro is the largest of Nova Scotia's towns and it is centrally located, which gives it the distinction of being "the hub of the province". As well as being an important centre of transportation, manufacturing, agriculture, trade and education, Truro is also well positioned for the future due to its location on the strategic corridor between Halifax and Moncton..

The town is experiencing a renaissance at the start of the 21st century with the renewal of many public buildings, including the fire hall and police station (both new buildings), and the civic building.

In addition, a new pool was built in Victoria Park and a new community workshop was opened. Plans for 2007 include a new hospital to replace the existing Colchester Regional Hospital and the Marigold Cultural Centre that will open downtown, transforming an abandoned movie theatre into a year-round, multi-use building.

Truro is served by six elementary schools, Truro Junior High (which opened in 2004) and, for grades 10-12, the Cobequid Education Centre. In addition, the Acadia School of Truro (Ecole acadienne de Truro) gives parents the option of choosing a French-based education for their children. There are several schools offering courses at the post-secondary level. They include the Nova Scotia Agricultural College, the Nova Scotia Community College (Truro Campus), the Institute of Human Services Education and the Success College of Applied Arts and Technology.

A municipal water treatment system serves the town and draws water from the Lepper Brook watershed. A sewage treatment facility known as the Central Colchester Wastewater Treatment Facility serves over 25,000 people in the town of Truro and the adjacent county. The treated effluent is discharged into the Salmon River and Cobequid estuary.

Perhaps Truro's greatest asset is Victoria Park, approximately 400 acres of natural woodland located in the centre of town. It dates back to 1888, when the core land containing Lepper Brook with its two sets of waterfalls and gorge, was donated by Susan Waddell Stevens. In addition to the paths that offer a quiet retreat to walkers, joggers, photographers, bird watchers and nature lovers, the park also contains a tennis courts, an outdoor swimming pool, a little league ballfield, a playground and water spray park, a bandshell, picnic tables and a cook-out pavilion. Kiwanis Park, a much smaller but very picturesque park, is located in the west end of Truro. It is the site of Fisherama, an event held each May for youths 16 and under.

The most common tree lining Truro's streets is the elm, but each year many of these stately trees need to be cut due to Dutch elm disease. Sculptors have been commissioned to turn the trunks of approximately 40 of these trees into art, to the delight of visitors and residents.

Truro is the only town that includes a First Nations reserve, the Millbrook Reserve. Although residents of the reserve do not pay taxes, they do pay for services from the town and consider themselves to be residents. In fact, a Millbrook resident was nearly voted onto council recently, losing by only six votes.

Why 7th?

A 26th for number of children was the poorest result; while a 23rd for growth over 5 years, and a 22nd for family income also had a negative effect on the overall result.

On the positive side, a 1st for land base, due to Truro being the largest town in area as well as population, increased the town's overall standing. A 2nd for early town status, and 5th in both university educated population and single population were all helpful.

Sources

www.town.truro.ns.ca
www.nsac.ns.ca

Clockwise from top: Cenotaph with police station in background, Kiwanis Park, Colchester Regional Hospital, Downtown Truro sign and Via Rail station.

Clockwise from top: N.S.C.C.–Pictou Campus, Nova Scotia Museum of Industry with hydrant art and Town Hall.

8

Stellarton

Original Names

English: Stellarton, renamed from the original Albion Mines at a public meeting in 1870, after a high-oil content coal called Stellar, which was found here in abundance

History

Land was granted to Donald Cameron in 1775 and settlement was begun prior to 1789 by Donald McKay, Sr. Coal was discovered in 1798 and John McKay was doing some surface mining by 1807. In 1825 the Nova Scotia reserved mines were leased to the Duke of York, who gave the lease to Rundell Bridge and Rundell, Jewellers, in payment of debts. They gave it to the General Mining Association, whose stock they owned and, in 1827. the Association purchased Dr. McGregor's farm, began setting up equipment, built the Mount Rundell Mansion for their agent and began raising coal. By 1828 about 170 people lived in what was then known as Albion Mines.

The General Mining Association began mining ore in 1828 and, in 1829, a blast furnace was erected for making pig iron. Two blast furnaces were erected about 1893, but iron production was exhausted by the early 20th century.

One of the earliest railways in North America was constructed by the General Mining Association between Albion Mines and New Glasgow, going into operation in 1839. The Intercolonial Railway was completed in 1867 and a station was built in 1875. In 1904 the Egerton Tramway Co. Ltd. completed their tram line connecting Westville, Stellarton, New Glasgow and Trenton.

A postal way office was established in 1841 and a post office in 1852. Anglican Christ Church was consecrated in 1852. The first school was held in 1875, with Central School being built in 1899.

Stellarton's industrial enterprises in the 20th

century include Pictou County Dairy, formed in 1913; D. Porter and Son Ltd., who purchased the MacArthur Woodworking Plant soon after 1911; Wear Well Garments Ltd., which grew out of Stella Bedding Co. Ltd., a firm founded by Richard Chisholm about 1950; Donato, Faini & Figli (Canada) Ltd., an Italian textile firm whose plant opened in 1959; Scotian Fiberglass Products Ltd., and Clairtone of Canada, Ltd., whose plant opened in 1966.

The Foord seam is one of the richest sources of coal, but one of the most dangerous. From 1880 to 1957 a total of 650 miners lost their lives in Stellarton mines. In 1992 the Westray mine (in nearby Plymouth), which also tapped the Foord seam, ended in tragedy.

Stellarton Today

Stellarton is home to Empire Company Limited, the parent company of Sobeys Inc. and Atlantic Canada's largest company, with revenues of over $11 billion in 2005. This exceeds the total combined revenues of the next three largest companies. It is difficult to miss the Sobeys warehouse, but the head offices of Empire Company Limited are not obvious. This mega-corporation could have moved to central Canada, but the Sobey family are committed to Nova Scotia, especially Stellarton.

Two of Pictou County's largest employers, Sobeys and the Scotsburn Dairy Co-op, are located in the town and Nova Scotia Power has one of its three regional offices here. Coal mining continues with strip mining, but employment is very limited compared to the prosperity derived from this industry in the past. The railroad also continues to operate, but without the number of jobs provided by the CNR in the past.

Stellarton's water treatment system draws water from the East River, the largest river in Pictou County. The town is served by the East River Pollution Abatement Plant, a modern facility that provides sewage treatment to the four adjacent Pictou County towns and discharges into the East River. Due to careful planning, the Trans-Canada Highway travels through Stellarton and, even after the twinning of the highway, the town has easy highway access.

G.R. Saunders Elementary is located within the town and offers grades primary–six, while grades seven and eight are bused to Highland Consolidated Middle School in Westville. Grades nine–twelve are bused to Northumberland Regional High School in Alma. The Nova Scotia Community College (Pictou Campus) is based in Stellarton. The first phase of an $11 million expansion of the college included the addition of an attractive, curved, two-story new wing, enabling the college to serve an additional 365 students. It has tripled the size of its library and made it available to the public, as well as offering high school upgrading programs. For those interested in a university education, highly-rated St. Francis Xavier University is within commuting distance in Antigonish.

The Museum of Industry, Atlantic Canada's largest museum, is located at the entrance to Stellarton. It has many interactive displays and is open year round. The attractions include Samson, Canada's oldest steam locomotive, which once carried coal over the rich Foord coal seam that lies 1100 feet beneath the museum site.

Stellarton Town Hall, with its unique clock tower, is one of the oldest in the country, while the Public Library, located next to the Town Hall, is a branch of the Pictou-Antigonish Regional Library. The Aberdeen Hospital, a regional facility that serves Pictou County, is available in nearby New Glasgow.

Stellarton enjoys impressive recreational facilities including Allan Park, Albion Ball Field, Semple Ball Fields (two fields), Dorrington Fields (two fields), Evansville (two fields), Sobeys Soccer Complex (three fields) and the Samson Walking Trail. In addition, a new international-size track and field facility is being developed in the coal reclaimed area of the town on part of the 650 acres that is being given to the town by the province.

Why 8th?

Stellarton placed well in the overall ratings. Its poorest results were 22nd in both multicultural population and population density. The best results included a 7th place in both early town status and number of children, while an 8th place in both full-time earnings and climate for gardening also improved the overall placement.

Sources

www.stellarton.com
www.sobeys.ca
www.gov.ns.ca/moi/
www.nscc.ca/about_nscc/Locations/Pictou.asp

Clockwise from top: Post Office, G.R. Saunders Elementary School, Streetscape near Allan Park, Tree and Hydrant art on Foord Street.

Clockwise from top: Dinosaur Delight (puppets from a Mermaid theatre of Nova Scotia show), Age of Sail mural: depicts the bustling waterfront of 1910, Haliburton House: was the home of Thomas Chandler Haliburton, recognized as the first author of American humour.

9
Windsor

Original Names

Mi'kmaq: Pisiquid (the place where the tidal flow forks)

French: Pisiquid, the Mi'kmaq name was retained by the Acadians

English name: Windsor. In 1764 the township was erected under the name of Windsor after Windsor, England – the chief residence of royalty for many centuries

History

By 1714 there was an Acadian population of 337 in the area. Fort Edward was built by the British in 1750 for the protection and the more effective control of the area. In 1759 a grant was made to Joshua Mauger, Michael Francklin, Isaac DesChamps, Charles Porter, William Saul, Moses and Gideon Delesdernier. DesChamps lived in Windsor by 1761. Many of the first inhabitants were Presbyterians from the North of Ireland; tenants living on land owned by absentee Halifax landlords.

The Acadian church of L'Assomption stood near the site of Fort Edward, and was probably built in the early 18th century. An English chapel, which was also used for school purposes, was built around 1771. One of the earliest English schools in the town was begun in 1767, with Samuel Watts as school-master. Kings College was founded by an act of the Provincial Assembly in 1789 and stayed in Windsor until it was moved to Halifax in 1923.

The first agricultural fair in Canada was held at Fort Edward Hill in 1765. One of the first houses of entertainment was kept by William Sentell in 1768. The Clifton Hotel opened in 1860.

Windsor had an established post office beginning in 1786. "Clifton", the residence of Thomas Chandler Haliburton, built in 1836, was taken over by the Provincial government for restoration as a museum in 1940. The railway between Halifax and Windsor was completed in 1858.

Most of the main section of the town was destroyed by fire on the night of October 17-18, 1897. Loss was estimated at over one million dollars.

The economy has been based on fishing, shipping and shipbuilding, agriculture, and retail operations. Tourism has become a major seasonal industry in recent years.

Windsor Today

Windsor is known as "the birthplace of hockey", as well as the "home of Sam Slick" and "big pumpkin country". This draws distinction to this small town from the worlds of sport, literature and gardening. Located at the "gateway to the Annapolis Valley", and a short drive to Halifax, Windsor seems to have something for every interest.

Thomas Chandler Haliburton, a resident of Windsor in the early 19th century, left his legacy to the town. His residence, Haliburton House, is now the Haliburton House Museum, part of the Nova Scotia Museum, and draws thousands of tourists to Windsor each year. The author's fictional character, Sam Slick, known for such maxims as "The Early Bird Gets the Worm", "It's Raining Cats and Dogs", and "Quick as a Wink", is celebrated in a three-day festival every summer. In addition, his likeness can be found on street and entrance signs, although, to be fair, it could as naturally have been a hockey stick or a giant pumpkin.

Mermaid Theatre, Nova Scotia's world-class puppetry company has toured around the globe and is a major presence in Windsor. Their unique adaptations of children's literature have won them international recognition and they have earned Export Excellence Awards from both Nova Scotia and the Government of Canada in recognition for contributions to the Province's culture and economy. In addition, they travel throughout Nova Scotia each year performing their unique children's theatre and encouraging the art of puppetry.

Employment in Windsor is diversified, with the largest employer being the Hants Community Hospital. Avon Valley Greenhouses, based in nearby Falmouth, is the seventh largest greenhouse operation in Canada, and a significant employer within the region. Fundy Gypsum Company Ltd. is located outside Windsor and ships natural gypsum to wallboard plants in the Eastern United States and cement manufacturing firms in Ontario; it is another important regional employer. Finally, Ski Martok is located near Windsor and provides important seasonal employment.

Windsor has excellent public schools within the town that allow students to walk to school for their entire public school education. Several private schools are also located in Windsor. They include King's-Edgehill School, Canada's oldest private residential school established in 1788; Citizens of the World Montessori School; and Oakmount Academy.

A new library was built in 2004 with $800,000 raised by community volunteers. A new water treatment facility was opened in 2001 to serve the Town of Windsor, as well as Three Mile Plains. It draws water from Mill Lake. A sewage treatment plant was initially installed in the 1960s and upgraded in 1993/94, but in 2006 it serves only 50% of the town. It discharges into Trecothic Creek. Untreated sewage is currently discharged into the Minas Basin, but changes are planned, as the Windsor Town Council is reviewing treatment options.

The Hants County Exhibiton, held annually in Windsor since 1765, is the oldest continuous agricultural fair in North America. In more recent times, Howard Dill has established Windsor as the Giant Pumpkin Capital of the World and has been commemorated with a statue located in the downtown.

Why 9th?

Windsor placed well due to having no extremes. The lowest placement was 24th in affordable housing, with the next worst showing being a 21st for family income. An 18th place in both number of children and population density also had a negative effect on the overall standing.

A 4th place in both early town status and growth over 5 years, and a 7th place in single population all had a positive effect on the overall standing.

Sources

www.town.windsor.ns.ca
www.mermaidtheatre.ns.ca
www.birthplaceofhockey.com
www.howarddill.com
http://museum.gov.ns.ca/hh/

Clockwise from top: Windsor entrance sign; Howard Dill statue, with a hockey mural in background depicting a hockey player of the late 1800's; Fort Edward Historic Site that features the last surviving blockhouse in Nova Scotia and the oldest such structure in Canada; entrance to Kings-Edgehill School.

Clockwise from top: Mastodon Ridge, Stewiacke River with ball field in distance, Old post office.

10

Stewiacke

Original Names

Mi'kmaq: Esiktaweak (whimpering or whining as it goes along)

English: Stewiacke, evolved from the Indian name, and was called Lower Stewiacke until the post office dropped "Lower" in 1913

History

In 1812, 2000 acres of land on the south side of the junction of the Shubenacadie and Wilmot (Stewiacke) Rivers were granted to Thomas Ellis, senior and junior; George, John and James Ellis; and John Turner. In this intervale land, the settlement of Lower Stewiacke began. After the Intercolonial Railway was built on higher land further east, the centre of population shifted to the area around the station.

James Harper was schoolmaster at Lower Stewiacke in 1816-1817, and a schoolhouse was built before 1840. A postal way office was established at Lower Stewiacke about 1836, which became a post office in 1852. In July of 1913, the name of the "Lower Stewiacke" Post Office was changed to "Stewiacke".

A Baptist meeting-house was opened in Lower Stewiacke in 1812 and a Temperance Hall in 1877. A wooden bridge was built over the river about 1841, which was replaced by an iron highway bridge in 1893.

Ten buildings were destroyed by fire in the main section of the town on May 2, 1921; six families were left homeless after a fire on Main Street on October 30, 1923; and fire destroyed a blacksmith shop, the Town Hall and the C.G. Leck store on July 29, 1939.

The Dickie lumber mill was built in 1879 and operated until 1921. A shoe peg and shank mill was built by J. Lewis and Sons, and began operation in 1914. During W.W.II, weaving was carried on, and in the 1950's the plant was sold to the Canadian

Lumber Company. It was occupied by the Wolf Cap Company, and in 1959 was used by Federal Products Limited of Truro, manufacturers of cotton and woolen goods. Lumbering has always been a major industry, while the retail and service sectors have also been important.

Stewiacke Today

Many of us have driven on the Trans-Canada Highway, used the services at exit 11 and seen the mastodon at Mastodon Ridge without realizing that we were looking at the outer edge of the town of Stewiacke. The main part of the town is located nearby on the original Halifax to Truro highway. Known by the term "winding river" or "halfway between the north pole and equator", its location on the strategic Halifax-Moncton corridor provides this town with considerable growth potential.

As it is only 45 minutes to Halifax, many of the residents commute to employment in Halifax or Truro, while others find employment at Mastadon Ridge or with employers in the main part of the town. Realizing that the future prosperity of the town depends on attracting an industrial base, the town of Stewiacke has purchased 76 acres of land on highway 102 (the Trans-Canada) at exit 11 for an industrial park. This is a long term investment in order to build a strong commercial/industrial tax base, as currently the town is mainly residential.

Stewiacke is in the last phase of an improvement to its water treatment system, which draws water from the St. Andrews River. The town also has a modern sewage treatment system, which discharges into the Stewiacke River. Both systems were built to accommodate growth.

Tourism obviously has potential for growth due in part to the town's convenient location for travelers and its setting in the midst of the areas rivers and farms. A new Bed and Breakfast, The Nelson House, is a sign that the quiet charm of this small town has not gone unnoticed.

Recreation facilities include a park with a playground, ball fields, a soccer field and, in 2006, the construction of the John Crawford Trail will begin, to the delight of the town's walkers. A new elementary school is also being planned, which should help to attract young families to this small safe community. As it celebrates its 100th birthday in 2006, Stewiacke will have many reasons to be optimistic about the future.

Why 10th?

Stewiacke had excellent results in five of the categories, including a 1st place in the very important number of children. A 2nd place in population density and 5th place in growth over 40 years were strong placements. In addition, a 9th place in both full-time earnings and growth over 40 years further improved the overall result.

On the negative side, a 25th in university educated population, a 24th in single population, a 23rd for early town status, and a 22nd for employment rate all served to reduce the overall placement.

Sources

www.stewiacke.net
www.mastodonridge.com

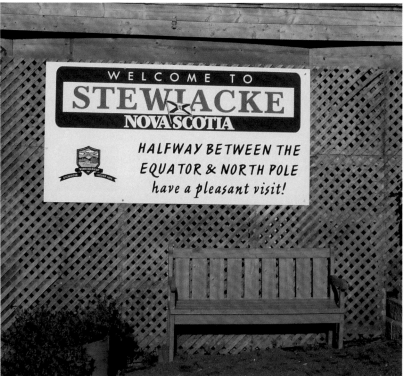

Clockwise from the top: Sign and bench at Mastodon Ridge, Playground at Dennis Park, The Nelson House, Dennis Park, Oldest house in Stewiacke. Opposite: Sign on Trans-Canada Highway

Clockwise from top: Acadia Park, War memorial and Westville Civic Building.

11

Westville

Original Names

English: Westville, replacing the name Acadia Village at a public meeting held in 1868 – probably because it was the westernmost of the East River mining towns

History

Coal was discovered here in 1866 and, in 1868, the Intercolonial Coal Company began developing land that they bought from John Campbell. The Acadian Coal Company began operations in 1866 and the settlement that sprang up around their works was named Acadia Village until a public meeting in 1868 renamed it Westville.

A postal way office was established in 1868 with Duncan Balfour as Postmaster. A school-house was opened in 1870, and in the same year Carmel Church was completed. An electric tramway connecting Westville, Stellarton and New Glasgow was constructed in 1904.

A railway was built to join the mines with the Intercolonial Railway in 1867-68. A railway built to the loading docks on the Middle River was opened in 1871. On May 13, 1873, an explosion at the Drummond Colliery killed sixty men and boys. The slope was not re-opened until 1875. Eventually three companies worked the seams of coal, with 1910 being the year of peak prosperity.

By 1959 about one hundred men were working at Drummond Collieries, in what was described as a dying industry. Public service industries and retail outlets accounted for most of the town's commerce.

Westville Today

Westville has traditionally been connected with coal mining, but today there is no coal mining within the town and most of its residents commute to work outside the community. Fortunately, Westville is one of the four Pictou County towns that together make up the third largest concentration of population in Nova Scotia and this provides significant employment nearby. Many find employment with large regional employers; including Empire Company, Sobeys Inc., Neenah Paper Inc., TrentonWorks, Michelin and Scotsburn Dairy.

Students can walk to Walter Duggan Consolidated for grades primary–six, and to Highland Consolidated Middle School for grades seven and eight. Grades nine–twelve are bused to Northumberland Regional High School in Alma. In addition, the recently updated Nova Scotia Community College (Pictou Campus) is located close by in Stellarton, and highly-rated St. Francis Xavier University is within commuting distance in Antigonish.

The town supplies water to its residents from the modern Forbes Water Treatment Facility, which was created by New Glasgow in 2000. The water is drawn from Forbes Lake, a designated watershed located in Pictou County. The town's sewage is treated at the East River Pollution Abatement Plant, a modern facility that discharges into the East River. It also serves the towns of New Glasgow, Trenton, and Stellarton.

Westville Public Library, a branch of the Pictou–Antigonish Regional Library, is located in the newly renovated Victoria School. It supplies a wide range of services as well as the latest in technology. The Westville Miner's Sports Centre is the home of hockey and skating during the winter; while the Pioneer Ball Field is home to summer sports, with the added benefit of night lighting. Another community attraction is Acadia Park, site of the Acadia Mine. It is an example of how land can be successfully reclaimed and returned to its former state. The park, opened in 1997, includes walkways, paths and trees, bridges, a playground and a pond. The park should be especially busy on Canada Day, as

Westville hosts the largest Canada Day celebrations in Atlantic Canada. The five-day event includes a giant street parade and features guest bands from around the world.

As this book is being prepared in early 2006, Westville's administrative affairs are being managed by New Glasgow's administrative staff. This situation should change as, within Pictou County, Westville is experiencing residential growth second only to New Glasgow. Of all Pictou County towns, Westville has the largest land area and therefore strong potential for continued growth.

Why 11th?

Westville had an impressive number of categories with high placements, while having a few that had a negative effect on the overall result. The poorest results included a 27th for university educated population, a 24th for family income, a 23rd for employment rate, and a 22nd for multicultural population.

Positive results included a 2nd place for number of children, a 5th place for affordable housing, a 6th place for land base, and 8th for both climate for gardening and population density.

Source
www.westville.ca

Opposite page, clockwise from top: Irving Big Stop (the first view of Westville from the Trans-Canada Highway), Post Office, Holy Name Church with collier bell, Attractive older home, Eagles Funeral Home, Highland Consolidated School, Mural of Acadia Collier.

Clockwise from top: Venus Cove, Scotia Ferry Look-Off and Post Office.

12
Mulgrave

Original Names

Mi'kmaq: Wolumkwagagunutk (lobster ground)
English: Mulgrave. In 1859, by act of the Legislature, the previous name was dropped in favour of Port Mulgrave in honour of the Earl of Mulgrave, lieutenant-governor of Nova Scotia – eventually "Port" was dropped.

History

Captain William Armstrong, a captain in the British Army during the Revolutionary War, came to this area about 1785, and 800 acres of land were surveyed for him in 1789. James Cowie, a Scottish soldier, also located at Armstrong Cove about this time.

About 1819 Hugh McMillan established regular ferry service across the Strait. A school-house was built about 1848, with Jane Giles as the teacher. St. Andrew's Anglican Church was consecrated in 1852. A post office was established in 1856.

In 1861 W.H. Wylde moved here and built an estate. The cove became Wylde's Cove, until it was changed by an act of the Legislature in 1859 to Port Mulgrave in honour of the Earl of Mulgrave, Lieutenant-Governor of Nova Scotia.

In 1882 the railway was opened to Mulgrave and, in 1893, barges began carrying rail cars across the Strait. Until 1955, when the Canso Causeway was completed, the ferry service was the main industry along with employment from services such as stores and service stations. Fishing has remained a basic industry.

Mulgrave Today

Mulgrave, the mainland terminus for ferry traffic to Cape Breton prior to the building of the Canso Causeway, is too easily missed by travelers on the Trans-Canada Highway, but a turn onto route 344 will bring you quickly to this attractive hillside community that overlooks the Strait of Canso and Port Hawkesbury on the opposite shore. It is known as "a deep water port", and is ideally located for business associated with Nova Scotia's offshore oil developments. Indeed, the Rowan Gorilla I underwent a major refit at the Mulgrave Marine Terminal. Recently, the Strait Superport spent $5 million to construct a 48,000 square foot building to serve as a supply base to further develop the infrastructure.

Fishing had historically provided many jobs, but a downturn in the industry encouraged Mulgrave to diversify and focus on new and innovative industries, especially those that were attracted by the town's marine-related assets, such as the Mulgrave Marine Terminal and Venus Cove area. The town also has the benefit of being one of the largest geographically, and this large land mass is in close proximity to the waterfront.

Ocean Nutrition Canada, a division of Clearwater Fine Foods Ltd., is the town's major employer. It develops and markets omega-3 fish oil dietary supplements to customers located primarily in the United States, Europe and Asia. The company recently completed a $21.5 million expansion of its Mulgrave processing and manufacturing facility. Other major employers include Mulgrave Machine Works, and East Coast Hydraulics & Machinery Ltd.

Mulgrave upgraded its water treatment plant in 1999 and installed a new sewage treatment plant in 2001. The sewage treatment plant is located at the base of the Marine Industrial Park and was designed to serve both industrial and residential needs. It provides primary treatment and the effluent is discharged into the Strait of Canso.

Students can walk to the Mulgrave Memorial Education Centre that serves the educational needs of primary through grade eight, while high school students are bused to a regional high school in Port Hawkesbury. The Mulgrave Professional Development Centre is available within the town for the lifelong learning needs of residents as well as the technology training requirements of business and industry. In addition, a branch of the Nova Scotia Community College is located in nearby Port Hawkesbury, while highly-rated St. Francis Xavier University is located a short drive away in Antigonish.

The town has recreational resources that include parks, tennis courts, athletic fields, and an outdoor swimming pool. The Eastern Counties Regional Library, with seven branches in Inverness, Richmond and Guysborough counties, has its headquarters in Mulgrave.

Tourists are attracted to the Annual Scotia Days Festival that is held during the third week of July and features a variety of events that include a parade and fireworks. To add to the appeal of this quiet seaside community, a new museum, in the shape of the Scotia Two train ferry, is being built to celebrate Mulgrave's rich history as a ferry terminus.

Why 12th?

Mulgrave had both very high and very low results that produced a reasonable overall placement. The low results included a 30th for early town status, and 29th in both university educated population and multicultural population. A 28th for growth over 40 years and a 27th for family income also reduced the overall placement.

The positive side included a 1st in population density, a 2nd for land base, and 3rd in both employment rate and number of children.

Sources

www.townofmulgrave.ca
www.straitsuperport.com
www.ocean-nutrition.com

Clockwise from top: Venus Cove Park and Playground, Eastern Counties Regional Library, View of Strait from Scotia Ferry Look-Off, Ocean Nutrition, Strait Superport's new supply base building and Stora across the Strait.

Clockwise from top: Waterfront, Osprey Arts Centre and Container loading at the port.

12

Shelburne

Original Names

Mi'kmaq: Logumkeegun or Sogumkeagum (a canal cut through a sand bank)
French: Port Razoir, due to the shape of the harbour
English: Shelburne, replacing the name Port Roseway, the new name was given by Governor Parr in 1783 after the arrival of 3000 Loyalists – in honour of the Earl of Shelburne

•Shelburne

History

An association was formed in New York in 1782 for the purpose of establishing a settlement of Loyalists at Port Roseway. In 1783 approximately 3000 people arrived in thirty ships to begin the settlement of Shelburne. In a few years the town had grown to a population of approximately 16,000 (including 2000 black Loyalists), becoming one of the largest communities in North America, but when government rations were stopped in 1787, most of the population moved away. It remained as a large fishing and trading village.

The earliest church, Anglican Christ Church, was consecrated in 1790, while 12 schools had been established by 1791. A post office was kept as early as 1783, and a post office building was constructed in 1908.

A lighthouse was built in 1787. A railway station, to serve the newly constructed Halifax and South Western Railway, was built in 1905 and 1906. The Roseway Hospital, which was built for the Royal Canadian Navy during World War II, was obtained by the provincial government and opened in 1946 to provide increased facilities for Tuberculosis patients as well as general hospital facilities for the area.

The economy has been based on the fishery and on wood products, with tourism being a relatively recent development.

Shelburne Today

Shelburne is known as the "Loyalist landing", which serves to emphasize its rich historical connections. It is located on one of the world's best natural harbours, so it is only natural that the Mayor should describe it as "a seaside town". The town is currently working to establish a new ferry link between Shelburne and Boston, which, if successful, would dramatically increase seasonal traffic. This would benefit the tourism and retail businesses that are already an important part of Shelburne's economy.

This is a beautiful small town that has been used as a movie set. This is the reason for the lack of overhead wires in the central business district, which allows the visitor to step back in time. In addition, the town government has preserved the views of the harbour, and a new marina helps to make the waterfront accessible.

Upgrades to the inadequate town water system have been delayed due to funding problems, but the sewage treatment system serves the town well. The Roseway Hospital is located one kilometer from Shelburne and serves regional needs. Support from a former resident enabled the town to build an excellent library. The Osprey Theatre has also added to Shelburne's cultural life.

The town took over port management from the Federal government and has been successful. Continental Fine Foods, owned by Clearwater, is the anchor tenant. The Shelburne School for Boys, a major provincial institution, was closed recently. Finding new uses for this asset has been difficult. Although economic management is seen as a strength, economic development is perceived as the biggest challenge facing Shelburne.

Why 12th?

Shelburne's rating was helped by placing 1st in employment rate and climate for gardening. A strong placing at 6th for population density, and a 7th for single population also added to the placement.

There were two poor placements at 29th and 26th with both relating to population change. A 24th placement in early town status also lowered the overall standing.

Sources

www.auracom.com/tnshelb/
www.historicshelburne.com

Above: Shelburne at dusk.
Opposite page, clockwise from top: Dory Shop, Continental Seafoods, Harbour, Shelburne Harbour Yacht Club, Sailboats and Harbour at dusk.

Clockwise from top: Lahave River from Shipyards Landing, Kinsman Field and Town Hall.

14

Bridgewater

Original Names

French: La Have, for the general area
English: Bridgewater, after a community was established by 1815 at the main bridging point of the La Have River

History

In the late eighteenth century, German people from Lunenburg and Lower La Have moved into the area of the main bridging point of the La Have River. The community expanded after 1815, with a postal way office being established in 1837, followed by a post office in 1845.

The Union Church was built in the 1830s, and Mrs. Calvin Wheelock taught one of the earliest schools in the church. A school building was constructed in 1837 and by 1899 there were five schools.

The Nova Scotia Central Railway was completed in 1889 and, in 1902, Bridgewater became a station on the Halifax and South Western Railway being built between Bridgewater and Yarmouth.

Francis Davison became Bridgewater's first Mayor in 1899. In the same year, a major fire destroyed fifty-five buildings, including forty-three stores, the post office, two banks and the Opera House.

The Dawson Memorial Hospital was first opened in 1920, followed by a newer hospital by the same name that opened in 1966. The Bridgewater radio station, C.K.B.W., began broadcasting in 1947, and the Des Brisay Museum was built in 1965.

Retail establishments have historically comprised the main part of the economy, along with considerable shipping of lumber and pulpwood from the surrounding area. Recently the industrial sector has increased.

Bridgewater Today

Bridgewater is known as "the Main Street of the South Shore" for several reasons. It is certainly the regional centre for Lunenburg County and its retail sector draws from a wide area of the South Shore. It is also a regional traffic hub. With major developments in Bridgewater and nearby, the road system, which is a town responsibility, will require additional maintaining and upgrading. In addition, traffic logistics are increasingly becoming a challenge.

The Lahave River that flows through Bridgewater allows large ships to come in from the Atlantic as far as the bridges. The town owns a number of river properties and hopes in the future to make better use of its waterfrontage. In a town already made attractive by a large amount of green space, Bridgewater Woodland is especially noticeable, containing 24 acres of woodlands, a pond, showcase gardens and the DesBrisay Museum, the oldest municipally-owned museum in Canada.

Bridgewater, along with neighboring towns and the county, created the Enviro Program, which was subsequently named and extended province-wide by the Nova Scotia government. Environmental concerns continue to be important here with this being especially apparent with recycling at fast food outlets.

Employment is somewhat diversified, but Michelin is the major employer within the region. Other employers include ECI, Bowater's Oakhill Mill, Grant Thornton and the South Shore Regional Hospital. The service and retail sectors provide a significant percentage of employment.

A new water treatment plant was built five years ago. It draws water from local lakes. A 12-year-old wastewater treatment plant replaced an older system that had been in operation for 20 years. The river has been protected for many years.

A new justice centre is being built in Bridgewater and will have all services under one roof. The need for a large recreation facility continues, since plans to build a new 20 million dollar facility that was to include a pool, were side tracked by a disagreement over its location. Recreation, sport and cultural activities are strongly supported by the community. A new library is also needed and being planned. Volunteerism continues to be a strength for the town and has allowed it to do much more than would otherwise be possible.

Why 14th?

Bridgewater did well in the population change categories by placing 3rd in both growth over 5 years and growth over 40 years. It placed 7th in both land base and multicultural population, and 11th in employment rate. All of these placements improved the overall score.

The most negative results were 25th in affordable housing and 23rd in both number of children and population density. Placing 20th in both early town status and single population further weakened the overall result.

Sources

www.town.bridgewater.ns.ca
www.michelin.ca

Floating docks at Shipyards Landing

Clockwise from top: Veterans' Memorial Bridge, Michelin, Veterans' Memorial Park, King Street Court, A fall afternoon at Bridgewater Woodland Gardens, Old Bridge and DesBrisay Museum.

Clockwise from top: gazebo, Kings Mutual building and Berwick entrance sign

15

Berwick

Original Names

English name: Berwick, 1851, after the town of the same name in Maine, but not until it had been called Congden Settlement, Curries Corner, and Davison's Corner – all for early settlers

•Berwick

History

David Congdon settled here in 1810 and built a small house. About the same time, Enoch Congdon and David Shaw moved here from Phinney Mountain, Annapolis County. They were joined by William Davison about 1835, and it became known as Davison's Corner with a total of three houses.

In 1828 the Pleasant Valley Baptist Meeting House was built and was the home of the Second Cornwallis Baptist congregation until a new church was built in 1857-1858. A log school-house was probably erected prior to 1830, while another school, with its second floor used as a temperance hall, was built in 1850. Soon after this, Miss Fields opened a boarding school for girls. It closed after a year, but reopened in 1858 in Wolfville, as the beginning of the Acadia Seminary.

A postal way office was established in 1856 and it became a post office in 1858. The Windsor and Annapolis (later D.A.R.) Railroad was completed in 1869.

Arthur E. Bezanson established the Berwick Bakery in 1924; while Hayden Furniture Ltd., furniture repairers and manufacturers, started about 1949. H.D. Larsen, meat packers, began operations in 1947. The retail sector has also been important to the town, and supports the agricultural economy of the surrounding area.

Berwick Today

Berwick promotes itself as "the apple capital of Nova Scotia", but it could also describe itself as "the small town with a lot to offer". Many people obviously agree, as it is the fastest growing town in Nova Scotia at a time when many towns are losing population.

This is one of only five towns in Nova Scotia that has its own electrical utility. It enables Berwick to offer lower taxes, as well as allowing residents to enjoy lower electrical rates. The lack of a water utility may be perceived as a weakness, but residents have their own wells and there is an ample supply. The sewage treatment system is modern and discharges into the Cornwallis River.

Larsen Packers, the largest employer, also provides significant employment within the region. Michelin, another major regional employer is located nearby. Many residents are employed in Berwick's active retail and service sector. Although the hospital was closed, the building is the location of the health centre and the Annapolis Valley Regional School Board. In addition, military families often choose to live in Berwick and commute to nearby Greenwood.

This is a Valley town with a friendly population that boasts excellent amenities and strong service clubs. While there is a high percentage of seniors and active seniors groups, there is also a high proportion of young families that benefit from Berwick and District School, an attractive facility built in 1990. When the town needed to replace its aging rink, they turned to local business for part of the cost. The Larsen family contributed $100,000 for the curling component. Kings Mutual, an insurance company with roots in Berwick, contributed $1,000,000 of the total cost of $9,000,000. The Kings Mutual Century Centre will be built near the school and will feature an ice surface, curling rink, fitness centre, library and outdoor pool.

Tourism is starting to grow due to the combination of an attractive town and many activities.

Although there are no hotels, Berwick now has three beautiful Bed and Breakfasts. Over the Labour Day weekend, the town is busy with Berwick Gala Days, a three-day event that has been celebrated for sixty years and draws many visitors to Berwick. The money raised is used for youth activities.

Why 15?

Berwick did well in the categories of growth over 5 years and growth over 40 years by placing 2nd in both. Also helpful in bringing up the overall placement were a 7th place in full-time earnings and an 8th place in university educated population.

A 30th place for early town status, a 24th place for single population, and a 23rd place for affordable housing all had a negative effect on the overall placement. Although positive categories are perhaps more important than the negative ones, the rising cost of a dwelling is a concern.

Sources

www.berwicknovascotia.com
www.kingsmutual.ns.ca
www.michelin.ca

Clockwise from top right: Berwick Art Gallery and RCMP signs, Bargain Harleys, Larsen meat packing plant, the Hidden Gardens Bed and Breakfast and Berwick and District School. Opposite page: Western Kings Health Centre.

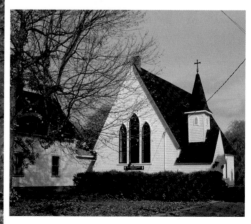

Clockwise from top: Town Hall, All Souls Anglican Church, Attractive house with fall leaves that was once the home of Mayor Freeman Porteous.

16

Oxford

Original Names

English name: Oxford, originally known as Head of the Tide. Although probably inspired by Oxford, England, it is a reference to this location as a convenient one for oxen to ford the river.

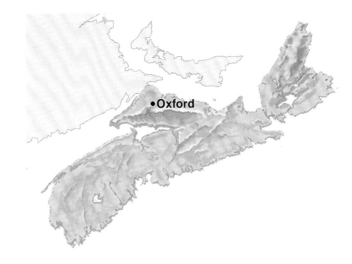

History

One of the early settlers was Richard Thompson, who bought from William Allan 1500 acres of land where the town now stands, and built the first sawmill there. Other early settlers included Joshua Reid, John Tait and Dalton Dixon. In the early 1800s, Oxford was known as Slab-town due to the abundance of sawmills and slabwood in the area.

A Methodist church was dedicated in 1855 and a new school house was erected in 1875.

Oxford was a flourishing manufacturing town for several decades after the Intercolonial Railway was opened in 1876. In 1867, the Oxford Woolen Mills were established. The Oxford Furniture Company Limited was started in 1873 and the Oxford Foundry and Machine Company was built in 1883. The Woolen Mills stopped production in 1953 and were liquidated in 1961. The Oxford Desk Company was liquidated in 1965. Its plant was taken over by Stanfields Limited to establish a knitting mill.

Oxford Today

Oxford is known as "the wild blueberry capital of Canada". This is an appropriate description as Oxford Frozen Foods, an international supplier of frozen blueberries (as well as carrots and onion rings), and one of Cumberland County's largest employers, is located in Oxford . The town established the Wild Blueberry and Maple Centre as a showcase for the maple and blueberry industries, which are centered on Cumberland County. The Centre is also an attraction for Oxford's fledgling tourism industry.

When the Trans-Canada Highway was relocated and no longer passed directly through Oxford, some businesses were established on the edge of town to serve the traveling public. The downtown readjusted to the reduced traffic, with surviving businesses serving the needs of the residents. Nearby Amherst, a major commercial centre, provides additional services.

Oxford is now a quiet, small town, with three rivers running through it. These are the Black River, River Philip and the Little River. The rivers are the reason for the location of the town and add to its beauty. Unfortunately, they can be dangerous during times of flooding and, as much of Oxford is on low land, it is cause for concern.

A new water treatment system was built in 2001 and draws high quality water from four wells. It is essentially the same source that provides Amherst with its highly rated water. The sewage treatment system is a modern system that was built in 1994, and discharges into the River Philip. The elementary and high schools are both old, but a new P-12 school will open in September 2009. This should help to attract more young families that are needed if the town is to grow.

Oxford benefits from its location on the strategic Halifax–Moncton corridor. It is also attractive to new employers, because of its clean environment. These advantages should also draw new residents, but house prices are higher than nearby towns, so many people commute to employment in Oxford. This is a challenge that is being addressed by the town, as they seek ways to make more affordable housing available.

Why 16th?

Oxford was brought down in the overall ratings by placing 26th in full-time earnings and 24th in single population. Placing 22nd in both early town status and multicultural population further weakened the overall rating.

Placing 4th in population density moved Oxford up in the ratings, as did an 8th place in employment rate. A 9th place in affordable housing and a 10th place for land base strengthened the overall placement. Although Oxford may not seem affordable when compared to neighboring towns, it is affordable when all 31 towns are being compared.

Sources

www.town.oxford.ns.ca
www.oxfordfrozenfoods.com

Above: Park next to the Black River
Opposite page, clockwise from top: Oxford Frozen Foods; GJDE, a unique store that draws shoppers to Oxford, is housed in an historic building that once acted as a movie house for the town; River Philip, known for the best salmon fishing in the area; An attractive house that was built in 1870, and is the home of Councilor Peter Swan whose family has owned it since 1902; Wild Blueberry & Maple Centre, which opened in the fall of 1998 in the former Scotiabank building; Wild blueberries carved out of a tree trunk.

Clockwise from top: St. John's Anglican Church, World War I monument and Golf club.

16

Lunenburg

Original Names

Mi'kmaq: Aseedik (the place of clams)
French (of Indian origin): Merliguesche (milky bay)
English: Lunenburg. Following a survey in 1753, it was decreed by the governor and council that the new settlement, which would soon welcome 1400 Foreign Protestants, would be named in honour of the royal house of Brunswick-Lunenburg

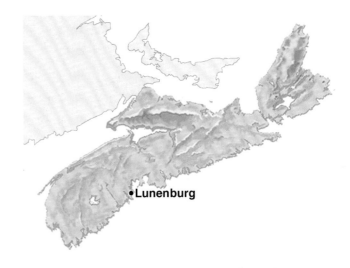

History

In 1753 the British government settled 1453 Foreign Protestants here; recruited from southwestern Germany and the Montbéliard district of France and Switzerland, these mostly German-speaking people were intended to help counter the French and Catholic presence in Nova Scotia.

St. John's Anglican Church, the second oldest church in Nova Scotia, was built in 1754. During both the Revolutionary War and the War of 1812, Lunenburg was raided by American Privateers.

Schools were established as early as 1754: the Lutherans obtained their own schoolmaster in 1760, and a school was erected for French-speaking people in 1775. A jail was built in 1753, a court-house in 1775, and a post office was established in 1819.

In 1820 the Fire Department started operating with an engine imported from London in 1819. By 1835 a public library had approximately 300 volumes. The Marine Hospital was built in 1879.

Fishing and ocean commerce have been Lunenburg's main industries, with Zwickers Co. Ltd. (salt fish producers, exporters and shipowners) established as early as 1789. Smith and Rhuland began their shipbuilding industry in 1900, and Lunenburg Sea Products began as W.C. Smith Co. in 1899. National Sea Products began operating in 1926. The Lunenburg Foundry and Engineering began in 1891, and Atlantic Bridge Co. in 1946.

Lunenburg Today

Lunenburg is best described as a "UNESCO world heritage site" or by the phrase "a proud past –

promising future". It is also the home port of the famous sailing ship Bluenose, which is pictured on the Canadian dime. The prosperity that the town experienced during its rich nautical history is still evident in its impressive architecture that dates from 1753.

Lunenburg has a water treatment system that draws water from Dares Lake, and provides an adequate quantity of quality water. The sewage treatment system that serves the town was upgraded to secondary treatment in 2003. It discharges into Lunenburg Front Harbour.

The historic Lunenburg Academy, which dates from 1895, provides elementary education, while Lunenburg Jr.–Sr. High School allows students to walk to school all of their public schooling. A community college is available in nearby Bridgewater, while several universities are within commuting range in Halifax and the Valley.

Lunenburg has a diverse economy that is based on the fishery, tourism, marine-related industries, manufacturing and IT. Highliner Foods (previously National Sea Products), one of the largest fish processing plants in North America, is located just outside the town limits. EADS Composites Atlantic, ABCO, and Lunenburg Industrial Foundry and Engineering (LIFE) help to provide a strong industrial base for the community. The Fisheries Museum of the Atlantic, part of the Nova Scotia Museum, was established as a Centennial project in 1967 to commemorate Atlantic Canada's fishing heritage. It is a world class tourist attraction, an important employer as well as being a major part of Lunenburg's waterfront.

A block of twenty-two buildings and eight wharfs on Lunenburg's historic waterfront were offered for sale by Clearwater Seafoods and purchased by the province of Nova Scotia in 2005. They will be turned over to the newly formed Lunenburg Waterfront Association, an initiative of the community, that will manage the sale of the individual properties so as to preserve the waterfront as a working marine-business district. The first company to move into the waterfront development was Lunar Fishing UK, a Scottish fishing company whose new fishing boat the Julianne III fits perfectly within the mandate of the Lunenburg Waterfront Association.

Lunenburg is also becoming a centre for the arts with nineteen art gallery owners forming the Art Galleries Association of Lunenburg. The Nova Scotia College of Art and Design (NSCAD) is exploring the establishment of an international arts institute within the town. A British oil executive, who owns a home in Lunenburg, has bought the Opera House with plans to restore it to a working theatre, rather than see it turned into something else.

Lunenburg is a small town that elicits strong loyalty from its residents, both old and new, who see it as a very livable place and work to maintain its quality of life. This was exemplified by the restoration of St. John's Anglican Church, dating back to 1754, after a devastating fire in 2001. The overwhelming community effort resulted in the restored building being rededicated in 2005.

Why 16th?

Lunenburg had several excellent results and several poor results, which averaged out to an overall rating in the middle. The worst placings were a 28th in the category for affordable housing and a 27th in number of children. A 26th place in population density and a 25th for growth over 40 years also served to reduce the overall placement.

Strength was shown by placing 1st in full-time earnings and a 1st in climate for gardening. A 4th place in university educated population, a 6th place for early town status, and a 7th for multicultural population were all also excellent results that improved the overall standing.

Sources

www.town.lunenburg.ns.ca
http://museum.gov.ns.ca/fma/
www.stjohnslunenburg.com

Clockwise from top: Lunenburg Academy, Touring by horse and wagon, Fisheries Museum of the Atlantic, Waterfront from across the water and One of the oldest homes in Lunenburg.

Clockwise from top: Amherst Industrial Park; War memorial and cathedral, both on Victoria Street

18

Amherst

Original Names

Mi'kmaq: Nemcheboogwek (going up rising ground)
French: Les Planches
English: Amherst, in honour of Lord Jeffrey Amherst,
who captured Louisbourg in 1758

History

The Acadians were first attracted to the area in 1672 and established their village, "Les Planches", on the site of the present town. The village was put to the torch in 1755 by the French. The area was resettled in 1761 by a group of New England Planters, Alpheus Morse, John Bent and Elisha Freeman. They were followed by immigrants from Yorkshire who arrived between 1772 and 1775. The first school was established in 1814, and the first church built was Baptist in 1818.

The community was transformed from a village to an industrial town with the completion of the Intercolonial Railway in 1876 and the development of the coal mining industry in Cumberland County. Early industries included the Amherst Boot and Shoe Company in 1875, the Canadian Car and Foundry Co. Ltd. in 1893, and the Hewson Woolen

Mills in 1902. In 1912 the McKay Auto Company moved to Amherst from Kentville. Standard Chemical Company Ltd. completed construction of a refined salt plant in 1947, and Bendix Home Appliances Canada Limited established an assembly plant in 1948.

Manufacturers located in Amherst in the mid 20th century included Canadian Assemblies Limited (license plates), Christie Trunk and Bag Company Limited, Dominion Manufacturers Limited (caskets), Elmac Co. Ltd. (insulating wool), Enamel and Heating Products Limited (aircraft components and parts, reinforcing steel, furnaces, bars and bolts), Maritime Pant Manufacturing Co. Ltd. (men's wear), Robb Engineering Works Ltd., Union Carbide, and Marden Wild of Canada Limited (tanning oils).

The Interprovincial School for the Deaf was

opened in 1961 and the Highland View Hospital in 1966. At this time Amherst was served by one radio station and one newspaper, the Amherst *Daily News.*

Amherst Today

The phrase "faith in our people – pride in our products" is an excellent description of Amherst, one of Nova Scotia's busiest industrial towns. Its strategic location on the Halifax to Moncton corridor, and in the geographical centre of the Maritime provinces, has been an asset to employers who have made it their home. Companies are also drawn to Amherst for its excellent water, which is said to be the best tasting water east of the Rockies. The September 2005 connection to natural gas, the first community outside Halifax/Dartmouth, gives industry another reason to consider moving to Amherst.

The investment of millions of dollars by Heritage Gas in an Amherst distribution system was only possible due to the support of an initial 331 customers (industrial, institutional, commercial and residential combined), who saw the potential cost savings and environmental benefits of burning Sable-produced natural gas. The mayor was quoted as saying that it would be much easier to promote the town as a community that offers alternative sources of efficient, environmentally-friendly energy.

Employment is currently well diversified. Major firms include Poly Cello and IMP Components. The Cumberland Health Authority is a major employer and TeleTech Holdings Inc. created 360 full-time jobs in September 2005 choosing Amherst as the location of their second call centre in Nova Scotia.

Amherst, as a regional centre, offers a wide variety of services. The Cumberland Regional Health Care Centre is a modern hospital that opened in

2002. Amherst Regional High School; E.B. Chandler Junior High; and Spring Street Academy, an elementary school that opened in 2005; are all modern facilities. The retail sector is strong as it draws not only from nearby Nova Scotia communities, but also from neighboring New Brunswick. In looking only at Nova Scotia statistics, it is easy to miss the fact that Amherst is a border town that includes parts of New Brunswick within its region. Mount Allison University, in nearby Sackville, New Brunswick, not only helps Amherst businesses, but also gives Amherst residents access to a university education.

The water distribution system draws water from the North Tyndal Wellfield. The high quality water requires little chlorination and is a source of pride for the town. Currently untreated sewage is discharged into the LaPlanche River, but a sewage treatment system is expected to be ready in 2006 and will provide secondary treatment.

The Amherst Wind Energy Project, the first of many wind power developments to be built on the Amherst Marshes, is projected to be operational by 2007. The 19 turbines will produce 31 megawatts, or enough energy annually to supply 10,000 homes. The Amherst RCMP moved into their new headquarters in 2005. It is located on the edge of town bordering the Amherst Marsh and gets 80% of its electricity from a wind turbine that is expected to have both cost and environmental benefits.

Volunteerism and involvement in the community is a trait shared by many of the residents of Amherst. This creates a welcoming environment for the newcomers that are being attracted by growing employment opportunities. It is always a challenge for small towns to compete against cities in order to attract young families seeking a place to establish roots and raise a family, but this town is better positioned than most in offering a small town lifestyle while attracting industries with high quality water, a central location, and both natural gas and environmentally sustainable wind energy.

Why 18th?

Amherst placed 29th in population density and 26th in median family income, which served to bring down the overall rating. A 24th place in full-time earnings further reinforces the need to increase the number of higher paying jobs. Also reducing the overall placement was a 22nd place in multicultural population.

    The best result was a 5th for employment rate. A 7th for early town status also improved the overall rating. An 8th place in both climate for gardening and, the very important, land base, served to move Amherst up in the overall rating.

Sources

www.town.amherst.ns.ca
www.heritagegas.com

Clockwise from top: Mural on side of building; One of the many fine homes in Amherst; Historic Pugsley's Pharmacy; Dayles Department Store, an Amherst landmark; The Town Clock Tower; Amherst downtown sign; Amherst RCMP Headquarters and Amherst Regional High School.

Clockwise from top: The Hawk Beach, Plover sign and Boardwalk.

19

Clark's Harbour

Original Names

English: Clark's Harbour, after Captain Jonathan Clark, an early settler

•**Clark's Harbour**

History

Barrington Township proprietors from Cape Cod and Nantucket in New England were the first settlers, arriving soon after 1761. A meeting-house was opened in 1838 and, at approximately the same time, a Free Will Baptist Church was built.

A postal way office was established in 1858 with Beverly Smith as office keeper, and a school-house was built in 1881.

Fishing has historically been the main industry. In the middle of the nineteenth century, the California Wharf and the Portland Packing Company sheds and wharf were put into operation. In 1947, Sable Fish Packers was begun by Basil Blades.

Clark's Harbour Today

Clark's Harbour, known as a friendly working community, is located on Cape Sable Island. This is a prosperous fishing community with the three largest employers being Clearwater Fine Foods, Sea Star Fisheries and Canus Fisheries. The work is demanding, but big money and big spending are not uncommon in the fishery. Shipbuilding has always been important, as this is the home of the Cape Island style fishing boat.

There is a friendly informality to the town with nicknames often used. A previous mayor was known as "Gomer" and a sports personality is known as "Blueberry". Sports are very popular and residents are not reluctant to drive the three hours to Halifax to see a game. Although the population is less than one thousand, volunteerism is high as the residents are heavily involved in the community.

Most services for the town are in nearby Barrington, on the mainland, but the community is served by a post office, bank, library, grocery store, restaurant, gas stations and building supply stores. There is no water system for the town, as residents rely on wells, but the sewage treatment system is very effective in protecting the environment upon which the economy is based.

The biggest challenge facing the town is the migration of the young to opportunities available elsewhere. Attracting young families is also the goal of many other Nova Scotia towns. Few towns have such a spectacular setting and this is enhanced by a 2000 foot boardwalk. Beautiful beaches are within walking distance, and tourism is slowly being developed, as the emphasis is on the working nature of this town.

Why 19th ?

Clark's Harbour was helped in the ratings by its location with a 1st place in climate for gardening. A relatively high birth rate yielded a 5th place in the number of children. A 5th place for high family income, and an 8th place for growth over 40 years also helped.

The town was hurt by 28th place in both land base and early town status. With no university nearby, a 29th place in university educated population is not surprising. It is inconsistent to see a 31st place in full-time earnings, while having a 5th place for median family income. This is the reason that I have two ratings for earnings, as one measurement is obviously not adequate.

Source

www.unsm.ca/chrbr.htm

Above: United Baptist Stone Church, The Hawk Beach and Dunes.

Clockwise from top: Cape Island boats, United Baptist Stone Church entrance and Church interior.

Clockwise from top: Lobster Rock wharf boats, Yarmouth street map and Yarmouth County Museum.

19
Yarmouth

Original Names

Mi'kmaq: Kespoogwit (land's end) for the area and Maligeak (crooked every which way) referring to the Yarmouth river
French: Port Fourchu (Forked Harbour)
English: Yarmouth, transferred from Yarmouth, Massachusetts, by New England planters and fishermen – it was in use as early as 1759

•Yarmouth

History

Sealed Landers and two other families came from New England and settled in 1761. They were followed by others and a small community was formed. In 1773-74 settlers arrived from Salem and Beverly, Massachusetts.

A post office was opened in 1896 and a Courthouse was completed in 1820. A lighthouse was constructed on Cape Fourchu in 1838-39. By 1821 there were two school-houses in the village.

In 1849 several families left for the "golden" West to seek their fortune. James F. Jeffrey found the "Runic stone" in 1897, which led to speculation of possible visits to the area by Norsemen around the year 1000.

Although direct rail communication with Halifax was established by 1891, and an airfield was built during World War II, it is shipping that has dominated Yarmouth's history.

Shipbuilding began as early as 1764, and in the nineteenth century expanded into an impressive merchant fleet. By the 1870s Yarmouth reached its pinnacle of fame and possessed more tonnage per capita than any other seaport in the world. All this was swept away by the advent of steam and the consequent decline of sail.

In 1887 the steamship *Yarmouth* began service from Yarmouth to Boston and, in 1956, the motor vessel *Bluenose* began service between Yarmouth and Bar Harbour.

Yarmouth Today

Described as "an historic seaport", this town has grown to become the regional centre of south western Nova Scotia, serving the needs of those living in the tri-county area of Yarmouth, Digby and Shelburne. As the Nova Scotia port for ferry crossings to Bar Harbor, Maine, Yarmouth is known as the international gateway to the province.

The last few decades has seen the need for change. The 1980s and 1990s saw the closure of several major employers and this was compounded by a downturn in the groundfish industry. This has forced the town to diversify by attracting new businesses, such as Regiser.com, which are being attracted by the quality of life and a workforce that has developed positive "can-do" attitudes.

Yarmouth's unique location has brought the advantages of being a natural port for a ferry service to the United States and Nova Scotia's earliest seasons, due to its southern location; but it has also brought the disadvantages of dependence upon the ferries and being considered remote from Halifax. This dependence upon a strong transportation system is exemplified in the air service, which once had passenger jets serving the airport, but now has no passenger or cargo service.

The fishery and tourism are the largest overall employers but, as a regional centre, Yarmouth derives considerable employment from provincial and federal offices located within the town. The Western Regional Health Centre is the single largest employer and is known for innovation. When the training of registered nurses was transferred to universities by the federal government in 1995, the hospital retained its student nurses through a program developed with the Université Sainte-Anne and Dalhousie. Still, there is a doctor shortage, with 3000 people unable to get a family doctor. This is currently being addressed by three new health projects.

The fifty year old system which supplies water to the town from Lake George is presently being updated. The harbour is now pleasant, as a sewage treatment plant was installed in the early 1990s and the dory races are again held there. As a further example of positive change and innovation, the Yarmouth YMCA recently installed 40 solar panels to heat their indoor swimming pool.

The services available far exceed what might be expected for a town of this size. All five banks maintain a presence here and the retail sector is undergoing considerable growth. The beautiful and well-maintained homes from Yarmouth's prosperous past, and the Yarmouth County Museum (one of my favourite places), are a pleasure for both resident and tourist. The area around Yarmouth is rich in natural beauty and ideal for recreation. Gardening here is enhanced by the fog, which is frequent, and is popular with tourists fleeing the heat.

Why 19th?

Yarmouth finished 31st in family income, 28th in population density and 24th in employment rate. This served to bring its placement down, while there were five ratings that brought the placement up. They were a 1st in climate for gardening, a 4th for single population, a 6th for number of children, 8th for growth over 5 years, and 11th for land base.

Sources

www.yarmouth-town.com
www.catferry.com
http://yarmouthcountymuseum.ednet.ns.ca

Clockwise from top: Interpretive Park with Regional Hospital in distance, Mariners Centre, Frost Park Lookoff, Clock on Main Street, Milton Horse Fountain and Mountain Cemetery Chapel .

Clockwise from top: View of bridge from Jubilee Park, Jubilee Park sign and Captain James Crosskill house.

21
Bridgetown

Original Names

English name: Bridgetown, an earlier name, Hick's Ferry, was changed in 1824 due to a bridge built over the Annapolis River

•Bridgetown

History

Captain Robert Bruce was given a large grant of land in 1763, which he called Henley Farm. Peter Pineo is the first to have built a house here, sometime between 1755 and 1782.

In 1822 Captain John Crosskill R.N. (1749-1826) owned the land known as Henley Farm and laid out the town along the banks of the river. He is regarded as the founder of the town of Bridgetown.

As early as 1771 John Hicks operated the first ferry and the community was known for many years as Hicks' Ferry. The first bridge was built about 1805, with replacements being built in 1870, 1907, and 1920.

In 1828 Joseph Howe said that Bridgetown "is also a seaport, and vessels of very heavy tonnage may come up the river and discharge their cargoes into its bosom, an advantage which, notwithstanding the difficulties of the bay and river navigation, is one of first importance".

In 1822 Enoch Dodge built a house, which was later used as a post office with his son as Post Master. Andrew Henderson opened a school in 1824 and a schoolhouse was built between 1831-1833. St. James' chapel was consecrated in 1829, and a courthouse was built in 1855. The county home for the "poor and harmless insane" was built in 1894.

Harry Ruggles was the first Mayor in 1897. Reeds Furniture began operations about 1858, and an iron foundry was begun about 1864. In 1881 Reed's Organ Factory was set up. The International Brick and Tile Company was begun in 1890. A vinegar factory was established by Graves & Company about

1909, and Acadian Distilleries Limited was established in 1951. In addition to the manufacturing done in the town, fruit growing has been a major industry in the area.

Bridgetown Today

Bridgetown describes itself on its signs as "a friendly town" and on its website as perhaps the "prettiest little town in Nova Scotia". During the age of sail it was an important shipbuilding and commercial centre due to a location that enabled shipping to have access to the Bay of Fundy. The prosperity that this brought to Bridgetown is still evident with elm trees shading well preserved Victorian homes and making this one of Nova Scotia's most attractive towns.

Currently, the town is coming to terms with the loss of Britex, a major employer for the region, that was located just outside Bridgetown. Nevertheless, Bridgetown still has some successful small businesses, such as Integrity Printing, and has attracted others, such as Interplay, which exports their playground equipment internationally. The diversity provided by small business is a strength that is lacking in communities with one major employer, and Bridgetown is now building with an emphasis on small business.

Queen Street is a very pleasant small town commercial district, but there is now a need to attract new businesses that can prosper in the changed business environment. Fortunately, Bridgetown offers a variety of services and the infrastructure is modern and capable of accommodating growth. The town water treatment system supplies potable water to its residents and parts of the surrounding communities. The water is gravity fed from two lakes located on North Mountain.

Sewage is fully treated before being discharged to the Annapolis River.

This is a nice, safe and friendly community to raise a family or in which to retire. The Town Clerk and the Town Project Coordinator both stressed their strong recreation programs, making it easy to keep kids active. Young families and semi-retired couples, especially those that want to start businesses, are deemed to be the ideal new residents.

Kings Transit serves this community, and it is easy to travel to other Valley towns. In addition, the Trans County Transportation Society uses a wheelchair accessible van and cars to transport residents to appointments, some as far away as Halifax. Due to the proximity, many who have been drawn to the attractions of nearby Annapolis Royal have chosen to locate in the more affordable Bridgetown.

Why 21st?

Bridgetown had a 1st place for growth over 5 years and a 3rd place in multicultural population. This helped the overall rating, as did 9th place in growth over 40 years and 9th place in population density. A 12th place in affordable housing also helped the overall placement.

The worst scores were a 29th for single population and 27th for employment rate. The land base was the only other negative rating at 25th.

Source

www.town.bridgetown.ns.ca

Bridgetown Watch and Clock, a successful small business.

*Clockwise from top: The bridge today;
Masonic Hall, formerly the Presbyterian
Church; Train station mural, Pub sign;
Town Hall, formerly the Post Office;
View of the town from North Mountain.*

Clockwise from top: Monument to William Hall, native of Hantsport and recipient of the Victoria Cross; Colourful playground fence; View of Minas Basin.

22

Hantsport

Original Names

Mi'kmaq: Kakagwek (place where meat is sliced and dried)

English: Hantsport. An earlier name, Halfway River, was changed in 1849, because the place had become the chief seaport of Hants County

History

Settlement began in 1789 when Edward Baker purchased 330 acres from Henry David Denson, cleared some land and built a house. He later moved, but in 1790 John Lockhart settled nearby and started a community.

A school was established at Half-Way River in 1812, with Hiram Smith as teacher. A building used for church, school and community hall purposes was probably erected soon after. A Baptist meeting-house was opened in 1830 and a postal way office was established in 1849. The first train went through on Christmas Day in 1869.

There is a memorial in Hantsport to William Hall, a native son of African descent, who won the Victoria Cross during the Indian Mutiny of 1857. A hall was opened for educational and "moral purposes" in 1861, with a seminary opened within it by C.D. Randall.

Newspapers published in Hantsport included the *Advance* from 1894 to about 1912, and the *Review* around 1916-1917. Milledge Oulton Memorial Library, located in the community centre, was opened in 1957.

Minas Basin Pulp and Power Company was incorporated in 1927 and Canadian Keyes Fiber Company began operations in 1933. Hantsport's main industries have been shipbuilding, shipping, woodworking, fruit processing and canning, farming, and tourism.

Hantsport Today

Hantsport is often overlooked, yet it has one of the best locations in Nova Scotia. It is a seaport, yet it is a Valley town that sits on the west bank of the Avon river in a tidal estuary. It can draw on the resources of nearby Wolfville and Windsor, and, although within Hants County, it borders Kings County. A quiet, yet busy town, it calls itself "a haven of hospitality"

Cooperation has enabled Hantsport to provide much more for their small population than otherwise would have been possible. In the late 1980s they partnered with Kings County to provide sewage treatment. In 2004, sharing the costs with the nearby Glooscap First Nation, they installed one of the most modern water treatment plants east of Ontario. Kings Transit currently stops at Wolfville, but a natural extension of this popular service will include Hantsport, Windsor and Three Mile Plains.

Employment is well diversified. Fundy Gypsum moves gypsum to Hantsport from their quarries east of Windsor by using the Windsor and Hantsport Railway. It is transferred onto waiting ships by one of the fastest ship-loaders in the world. This is necessary as the tides in the Minas Basin (the highest in the world) require ships to enter and leave Hantsport within a 4-5 hour period.

The largest employer is Minas Basin Pulp and Power Company, which uses recycled paper product collected in the Atlantic Provinces, Quebec and the eastern seaboard to produce paperboard. They also generate their own hydro-electric power from the St. Croix River and return the water back to the mill. CKF is a related company that produces disposable plates. Minas Basin Pulp and Power Company is a leader in the green economy and will receive government incentives as Canada struggles to improve its poor environmental record by rewarding its leaders in this area.

Hantsport does have challenges such as the need to upgrade water distribution pipes in some areas and the lack of a truck route for industries. The town is also investing in recreational infrastructure, as they wish to draw more young families. With the green spaces, walking trails and the comfort and safety of a small town, Hantsport provides a pleasant environment for young and old.

Why 22nd?

Hantsport has a relatively high family income, finishing 6th in this category. It was further brought up in the overall ratings by placing 7th for its university educated population, placing 8th for having a high number of children and placing 11th by having a comparatively large multicultural population.

A 31st in the category for single population and a 30th in the category that measures a town's land base brought down the overall placement. With four other categories yielding placements of 22nd or 23rd, placing 22nd overall seems appropriate.

It is important to look at those categories that pertain especially to your needs. For example, you might not be happy here if you wish to find other singles, but you are apt to be successful in finding young families. This is an important strength for a town and Hantsport's 8th place in this category was the best in the Valley.

Sources

www.hantsportnovascotia.com
www.minas.ns.ca

Clockwise from top: Historic Churchill House, Town Hall, Windsor and Hantsport Railway, William Hall Sculpture, Just Us Chocolate Factory sign, Valley Credit Union, Post Office.

Clockwise from top: Geothermal Park, Entrance sign to industrial park and Town Hall.

23

Springhill

Original Names

English: Springhill, a descriptive name that was given due to the number of springs contained within the original hill upon which the town is located

History

The earliest settlers came to the area in the 1820s with families named Hunter, Gilroy, Anderson, Boss and Mills. The first school-house was built in 1853, a mile from the present site of the town. A Methodist Church was built in 1863. By 1871 there were only five houses in Springhill.

Lodovick Hunter discovered coal here in 1834 and the General Mining Association secured a grant on one hundred and sixty acres in 1849, but it was not until 1873 that mines were formally opened on a large scale. In the same year, the coal company began railway lines to Parrsboro and Springhill Junction to facilitate the movement of coal. In 1884 the mines and railway were purchased by Montreal interests and operated under the name of the Cumberland Railway and Coal Company.

With the beginning of large scale coal mining, the community grew quickly and became a town in 1889. In 1891 the town suffered its first disaster, when a mine explosion killed one hundred and twenty-five men.

In 1956 a mine explosion killed thirty-nine men, which was followed in 1957 by a devastating fire that swept the town. A "bump" in 1958 claimed a further seventy-six lives. In this last disaster, twelve miners were rescued after six days of entombment and seven more were rescued two days later.

Dosco closed its mines in Springhill in 1958, putting most of the town's labour force out of work. In 1959 a new coal mine was organized, which employed one hundred men by 1964. The federal government built a prison and other companies were created that helped to stabilize the employment situation, including a woodworking plant and the Surette Battery Company.

Springhill Today

Springhill, described by its mayor as the "energy centre of Nova Scotia", was known for high quality coal and is now becoming known for geothermal energy. In 1989, Ropak, a plastic container manufacturer, became the first company in Canada to use geothermal energy by extracting it from water pumped out of Springhill's abandoned mines and using it to heat and air condition its plant. In 2005, Springhill's new civic centre used the same cutting-edge energy source for heating and air conditioning the building and to provide the rink's ice surface.

Employment in Springhill is well diversified. Ropak, Surette Battery and the federal prison are the largest employers, while the education, health and retail sectors are also important. The town is actively seeking new businesses for its Geothermal Industrial Park, especially smaller industrial and manufacturing companies. Its location on the strategic Halifax–Moncton corridor and in the geographic centre of Cumberland County, as well as access to geothermal energy, is now drawing attention to the town.

Springhill has been served by a modern sewage treatment system since 1994. A new 4.3 million dollar water treatment system will be operating in 2006. Providing five times the quantity of the old system, it is also expected to solve the problem of water quality that has been a problem in the past.

This is the home town of international singing star Anne Murray. To celebrate her achievements, the Anne Murray Centre was built in the town's cente. It is a major tourist attraction that, along with the Miners Museum, is the base of Springhill's tourism sector.

With a nursery school, two elementary schools and a junior/senior high school, it is possible to attend public school without leaving Springhill. In addition, the Nova Scotia Community College (Cumberland Campus) is located within the town and Mount Allison University in Sackville, New Brunswick, is only thirty minutes away. A modern hospital, All Saints Springhill Hospital, serves not only the residents of Springhill, but also neighboring communities.

The future looks bright, as Springhill has an excellent location and affordable real estate. Low cost energy is undoubtedly its biggest advantage, as the importance of geothermal is only now being realized. Wind power is moving ahead, with Vector Wind Energy Inc. installing a 1.2 megawatt wind turbine near Springhill in 2005. The town also has methane gas, whose potential is, as yet, untapped, and half of Springhill's massive coal reserves have not been mined.

Why 23rd?

Springhill's 30th place in employment rate was not helpful to its overall rating. A 29th in both multicultural population and growth over 40 years also had a negative effect, as did a 26th place for university educated population.

On the positive side, a 2nd place for affordable housing and a 7th place for early town status helped to bring up the overall rating. Also to Springhill's advantage is an 8th place in climate for gardening, a 9th place for land base and a 10th place for single population.

Sources

www.townofspringhill.ns.ca
www.annemurray.com/amc/index.htm
www.nscc.ca/about_nscc/Locations/Cumberland.asp

Clockwise from top: Dr. Carson and Marion Murray Community Centre, Post Office, An attractive home, Flowers growing in downtown Springhill, Entrance to the Federal Prison, Nova Scotia Community College and Springhill Miners Museum.

Clockwise from top: Town Hall, Heart shaped street sign and MacDonald Museum.

24

Middleton

Original Names

English: Middleton, adopted in preference to the previous name, Wilmot Corner, at a meeting of the inhabitants in 1854

History

The first settlers probably came to Middleton in the last two decades of the 18th century, but by 1834 only a few houses had been built.

Holy Trinity Anglican church was built in the lower town in 1787 and consecrated in 1791. A postal way office was established by 1855 and a newspaper, *The Scribe*, was published about 1892-1894.

The Nova Scotia Central Railway was built through Middleton about 1867-1868. Between 1902 and 1905 a railway was constructed between Middleton and Port Wade. A new Negro Baptist church was dedicated in 1910 on North Street. Soldiers Memorial Hospital was built in 1960, opening in 1961.

Retail stores have been the main employers in the town while fruit growing, along with other kinds of agriculture, has been the major industry of the surrounding area.

Middleton Today

Located in the middle of an agricultural hub, Middleton is called "the heart of the Valley" and this is further reinforced with their brilliant heart-shaped street signage. The town is one of the larger Valley towns and is halfway between Windsor and Annapolis Royal. Although agriculture is not as dominant now as in the past, many of the businesses remain focused on agriculture.

Employment in Middleton is well diversified. Kings Processing Ltd. has expanded with a new facility to process local market produce. Mid-Valley

Poultry Co-op provides government inspection for small growers of free-range livestock, and Farmers Dairy and TRA Foods are also significant employers. Soldiers Memorial Hospital, the two regional schools and a provincial community college provide medical and educational employment. Additional jobs are available in the service and retail sectors located in the downtown business core.

Middleton has a swimming pool, a renovated arena, a new library, tennis court, curling rink, bowling alley and several parks. An old horse raceway became Rotary Raceway Park. It features a half-mile track, baseball and soccer fields, a basketball court, horseshoe pits and a children's playground. Riverside Park is a seven-acre park along the banks of the Annapolis River that features scenic walking paths, picnic sites and easy access to the river for sports fishing enthusiasts.

Other attractions include the Railway Station Museum, and the Town Clock (one of three water clocks in North America). The Old Holy Trinity Church is one of the five surviving Loyalist Churches in Nova Scotia. A magnificent nightly sight is the dramatic swoop of as many as 500 chimney swifts into the tall chimney preserved in their honour at the high school.

As the highly recognized and well used location of many community activities, MacDonald Museum collects, preserves and exhibits Annapolis Valley history in the original community school house.

Middleton now has a new water treatment system fed by area wells. In the past, Lily Lake was the primary source, but today it serves only as a backup. The sewage treatment system, which discharges into the Annapolis River, has both primary and secondary treatment. It is getting old and a new system is now being planned.

This is an active town with an aging population.

It remains affordable for families and, therefore, compared with other Nova Scotia towns, has a relatively high number of children. With recreation programs featuring active living being offered to all ages, Middleton strives to meet the needs of both young families and seniors.

Why 24th?

Middleton placed 4th in multicultural population. The next best placements were 13th for population density and 14th in both family income and growth over 40 years. Placing 16th in the very important category of affordable housing and also 16th for number of children were also beneficial.

The overall rating would have been higher without a 31st place in employment rate. The only other negative placement was 26th for early town status.

Sources

www.town.middleton.ns.ca
www.macdonaldmuseum.ca

Opposite page, clockwise from top: Holy Trinity Church, Entrance sign, Soldiers Memorial Hospital, Attractive house and Affordable housing.

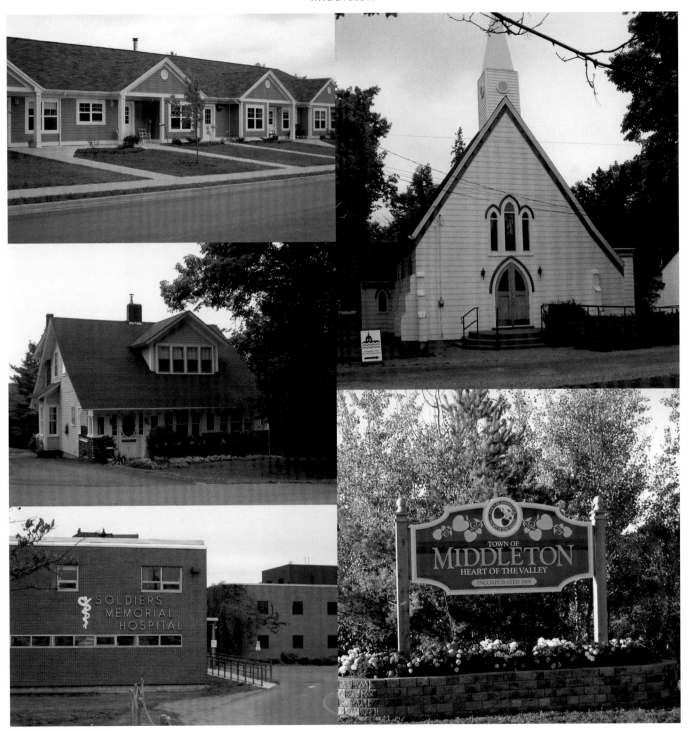

Clockwise from top: Fishing boats and Seafreez plant, Stanfest, Whitman House Museum and Tourist Bureau.

25

Canso

Original Names

Mi'kmaq: Kamsok (opposite a high bluff, or high banks opposite)
French: Campseau, Camseau, Canceau
Spanish: Ganso (goose)
English: Canso, several earlier names dropped in favour of Canso

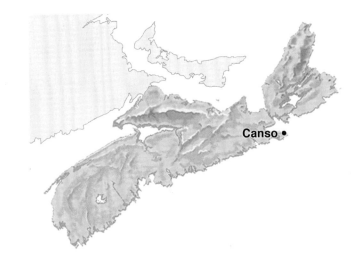

Canso •

History

In the 1600s the French used the area as a base for fishing operations. The English attempted to settle here, but Indian raids killed many of the settlers in 1720 and 1721. A blockhouse was built on Canso Hill by Edward How in 1735, but this, along with several houses, a store, three wharves, store rooms, and fish rooms, was destroyed by a French invasion in 1744.

In 1745, the fleet from New England assembled in the harbour on its way to attack Louisbourg. A blockhouse was built by the men and named Fort Prince William. In 1764 a town plot was laid out south of the present town and named Wilmot. During the American Revolution, privateers did considerable damage to the settlement and, by 1813, only six families remained. In 1814 a few families arrived and located at the Tickle. The town started to grow in 1821 and by 1844 there were two hundred and fifty families resident in Wilmot townships.

Mr. Peden taught school from 1736 until 1743, and a public school-house was erected in 1847. A lighthouse was built on Cranberry Island in 1817-1818. A Congregational Meeting House was completed in 1824. A postal way office was established in 1834 and in 1853 a post office was built.

A riot between Irish Catholics and Orangemen upset the peace of the village in 1835. The Great Storm of 1873 demolished many wharves and stores, Wilmot Hall, a Baptist Church and many vessels. Between 1881 and 1894 several transatlantic cables were landed here and Canso became one of the main communication links between North America and Europe.

An ice merchandising business was begun by James Hart in 1867. Around the same time, a lobster canning factory was established under the management of Alfred Ogden. A frozen bait storage plant was built by A.N. Whitman around 1903-1905. In 1910 the Whitman Fish Company sold out to the Maritime Fish Corporation. The Robinson Glue Factory was erected in 1910. The British Columbia Packers Ltd. plant was purchased by Acadia Fisheries Ltd. in 1963 and, in 1965, the first section of the new Acadia Fisheries plant was nearly complete. Fishing has historically been the major industry in Canso.

Canso Today

Canso's strategic location enabled it to prosper more than most during the dramatic growth in Canada's fishery after the extension of our territorial waters to two hundred miles, but the large ships departed (along with National Sea Products) prior to the collapse of ground fish stocks. This left the town with a relatively underdeveloped inshore fishery, as the focus had always been on offshore fishing. With no other industries, the unemployment resulting from this collapse created a financial crisis that has threatened the very existence of the town and much of the financial support for the area's economy.

Known as the oldest fishing port in the Maritimes, Canso did not fade away quietly. Extensive media coverage of Canso's plight has made it a symbol of small town Canada and resulted in individual Canadians across the country sending financial support through the Friends of Canso website. This support, along with the determination of the residents to retain control of their own destiny by voting overwhelmingly to reject amalgamation with the Municipality of the District of Guysborough, has

convinced the province to work with the town to solve the current financial problems.

Canso residents have always had a strong work ethic, but now there is a healthy attitude shift that is creating a more diverse economy. The new DCI call centre has created 80 new jobs, while the Seafreez fish processing facility provides 80-140 seasonal jobs. The inshore fishery remains healthy and there are two new Bed and Breakfasts, a natural business for this picture postcard town.

The Stan Rogers Festival is going into its 10th year and draws 10-12,000 music fans to Canso each year. Conceived by Troy Greencorn and Chris Lumsden, members of the Canso Lions Club, on behalf of the town, the festival is an example of local ingenuity. By land, Canso is the most remote of the towns, and Nova Scotians may not visit unless it becomes a destination. The exposure resulting from the festival can bring in new residents and businesses.

The town has a diverse infastructure for its size, which is the result of much local effort in the 1960's and prosperous 70's and 80's. It was one of the first towns to provide its residents with a sewage treatment plant, which protects the pristine environment. It provides treated water with an upgrade scheduled for next year. Eastern Memorial Hospital, a medical centre with 3 doctors and a dentist, and a modern nursing home are all located within the town. Although the retail sector has suffered, Canso has a pharmacy, garage, Co-op store and restaurants.

High-tech may contribute to Canso's economy, as it did a century ago when the transatlantic cable that linked Europe and North America came ashore here. Currently Barrington Wind Energy are establishing a $34-million wind farm in the town of Canso. This will not only contribute to the economy during the construction phase, add to the tax base, and attract business to the industrial park, but will give the town access to the electricity, since it is one of the few towns that has its own electric utility.

Why 25th?

Canso ranked 1st in affordable housing, and 5th in both population density and single population. A ranking of 6th in employment rate also helped in the overall standings.

The worst score at 31st in growth over 5 years comes as no surprise. A 29th place in full-time earnings was balanced by a 15th place in family income, as income can be measured a variety of ways. A 25th place in number of children is more of a concern.

Sources

www.townofcanso.com
www.stanfest.com
www.barringtonwind.com

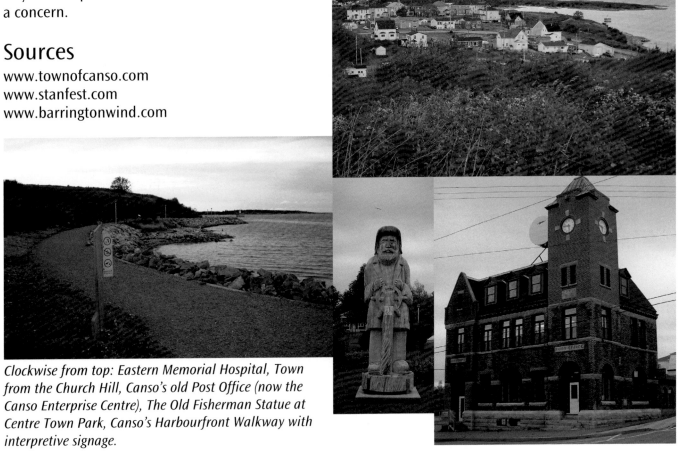

Clockwise from top: Eastern Memorial Hospital, Town from the Church Hill, Canso's old Post Office (now the Canso Enterprise Centre), The Old Fisherman Statue at Centre Town Park, Canso's Harbourfront Walkway with interpretive signage.

Clockwise from top: Trenton Municipal Airport, War monument with TrentonWorks in background, Trenton Civic Building.

25
Trenton

Original Names

English: Trenton, named after Trenton, New Jersey, USA, after being proposed by Harvey Graham in 1882 for the new town being laid out by him at Smelt Brook

History

The town site is on three lots that were granted (from north to south) to James Spry Heaton in 1786, to James McCabe in 1792 and to Roderick McKay in 1783. The Nova Scotia Forge Company was built in 1881 at present day Trenton, then known as Smelt Brook. In 1882 the Nova Scotia Forge Co. and other shareholders formed The Nova Scotia Steel Company. Also in 1882 they constructed the steel plant and a railway siding attached to it. The first castings were made at the N.S. Steel Plant in 1883. Harvey Graham purchased land from William Fraser on which he laid out the new town, house lots were auctioned off and, by the end of 1882, a number of houses and one or two stores were being built.

A school-house was established in 1883-1884 and a Temperance Hall was opened in 1886. First Presbyterian Church was dedicated in 1890.

Glass was made at Trenton in the late 19th and early 20th centuries. The Nova Scotia Glass Company was founded in 1881. The Lamont Glass Company was founded in 1890 at Trenton and in 1898 its plant was leased to The Diamond Glass Company. The Humphreys Glass Works was also established at Trenton in 1890, but moved to Moncton in 1890.

The Eastern Car Division's Railway Car Manufacturing Plant was built in 1912. The wheel plant was started in 1914, taken over by Dominion Wheel in 1915, bought by Canada Iron Foundries in 1952 and closed down in 1962. Trenton Industries Ltd. was incorporated in 1941. The Steel Plant railway car plant and Trenton Industries became the Trenton complex, controlled by Dosco. Tibbets Paints Limited was organized in 1947. The Nova Scotia Power Commision built a thermal generating plant about 1947, with an extension in 1960.

Trenton Today

Trenton, the birthplace of the first pouring of steel in North America, is an industrial town known primarily for its major employer, TrentonWorks, which draws approximately one third of its work force from the town. The town's motto, "strike while the iron is hot", is an accurate description of the town's prosperity. When rail cars are in demand and the plant is prospering, so is the town, but the opposite is also true. This applies, to a lesser extent, to all of Pictou County, since TrentonWorks is also its largest employer.

The other large industrial employer within the town is the Nova Scotia Power Generating Plant. Located next to TrentonWorks, it burns coal to produce electricity. In addition, many residents commute to work at nearby large regional employers; these include Michelin, Neenah Paper, Scotsburn Co-op Dairy, and Sobeys.

Trenton Library, a branch of the Pictou-Antigonish Regional Library, is located in the town; while the Aberdeen Hospital is in nearby New Glasgow. A modern water treatment system supplies water to Trenton from several deep wells. The sewage treatment system was created in the early 1970s and upgraded in the 1990s. It is now called the East River Pollution Abatement Plant, serves the needs of the four towns and discharges into the East River.

Two schools are located within the town: Trenton Elementary School (P-4) and Trenton Middle School (5-9). The North Nova Education Centre in New Glasgow provides grades 10-12. It is a modern regional high school that opened in 2003. The recently updated Nova Scotia Community College (Pictou Campus) is located nearby in Stellarton, while highly-rated St. Francis Xavier University is within commuting distance in Antigonish.

The Town of Trenton owns two impressive facilities: Trenton Park and the Trenton Municipal Airport. Trenton Park's 565 acres include century-old coniferous trees. Attractions include six kilometres of hiking trails, a two-kilometer mountain bike trail, a 3000 square foot swimming pool, and man-made ponds with ducks and stocked trout for fishing. The park also offers picnic sites, as well as serviced and unserviced campsites.

The Trenton Municipal Airport was started by a group of local flyers in 1929 and acquired by the town in 1950. It is classified as a "Local Commercial Airport" and is used by local small aircraft, charter and training companies, and corporate aircraft. Sightseeing and charters are available on helicopter and fixed wing aircraft. The facility includes two runways, a modern 3000 square foot terminal building, and a 10,000 square foot heated hangar.

Trenton lies beside the East River. Its homes often have views, as they are built into a hill that rises steeply above the massive TrentonWorks, which occupies much of the level land at the foot of the hill. Trenton Municipal Airport takes advantage of the level land at the top. The town benefits from being one of the four Pictou County towns that together make up the third largest concentration of population in Nova Scotia and this, regardless of the fate of its major employer, should guarantee Trenton a bright future.

Why 25th?

Trenton had poor results in a significant number of categories, which brought its overall rating down.

These included a 28th in university educated population, a 27th for early town status, and a 27th for growth over 5 years.

There were also positive results, which included a 4th for affordable housing, an 8th for climate for gardening, a 9th for number of children, and a 10th for single population.

Sources

www.town.trenton.ns.ca
www.parl.ns.ca
www.trentonworks.ca

Clockwise from top: Post Office, Nova Scotia Power's Trenton Generating Station, TrentonWorks, Trenton Elementary School, Trenton entrance sign.

Clockwise from top: Wildflowers in town, Town crest, Parrsboro Citizen Band Bandshell.

27

Parrsboro

Original Names

Mi'kmaq: Awokun (a portage, a short-cut, a crossing over point)

English: Parrsboro, after John Parr, who was Governor of Nova Scotia from 1782 to 1791

History

The Mi'kmaq came to the area for its unique geographical position and for the variety of minerals available. It is on the elbow of the Cumberland Pass and on the coast at one of the narrowest points on the Minas Basin. This meant that all those entering the Province with destinations in the present Truro and northern areas or in the direction of the Annapolis Valley and Halifax would find the Parrsboro route the most convenient. Travel by canoe was very convenient due to a suitable chain of lakes and rivers.

The original setting of the town that was to become Parrsboro began some two miles southwest of the present site, at Partridge Island. As early as the 1730's, two Acadian boatmen, John Bourg and Francis Arseneau, operated a ferry service across the basin from Partridge Island. With the expulsion of the Acadians in 1755, it became necessary for the British to re-establish this important link.

The "New England Planters" arrived and among the grantees in1776 were Avery, Bacon and Lockhart, on the condition that they run a ferry from Partridge Island to Windsor for fifteen years, capable of carrying passengers and cattle. Although the area was not as suitable for agriculture as other areas settled by the "Planters", it was ideal for lumbering, ship building and commerce.

Following the death of James Ratchford, a prominent merchant, there was a move from Partridge Island to nearby Mill Village. Sir Charles Tupper bought the Ratchford home on Partridge Island, calling it Ottawa House and using it as a summer home.

In the later half of the nineteenth century Parrsboro enjoyed unprecedented growth and prosperity as it sat at the crossroads of the country's major land and sea routes and could supply the timber, coal, iron ore, manpower and ships that were in demand. For eighty-one years (1877-1958) the Springhill and Parrsboro railway moved Springhill coal to world markets through the busy port.

Parrsboro Today

As you enter Parrsboro a sign announces "small town big heart"; it has also been described as the "gateway to the Bay of Fundy" and "Nova Scotia's best kept secret". Although this is not the most remote town, and it was historically on the main route between Amherst and the Valley towns, it is now seen mainly by residents and those for whom it is a destination.

Parrsboro is located on the Bay of Fundy and surrounded by natural beauty. Not surprisingly, tourism has become an important source of employment. The Fundy Geological Museum was built here in 1993 as a branch of the Nova Scotia Museum. It focuses on the geological history of Nova Scotia's Fundy region and welcomes thousands of visitors each year that come to see evidence of the dinosaurs that once roamed the area, as well as the many minerals still found on the shores of the Bay of Fundy.

Another major attraction is The Ships Company Theatre, which is dedicated to the production and development of Canadian and, especially, Atlantic Canadian productions. Their first play was performed on the MV Kipawo in 1984 and their new theatre, of which the ship is still a part, opened in 2004.

The hospital that closed in 1995 became the South Cumberland Community Care Centre. A Medical Clinic was opened nearby in 1999. Parrsboro Regional Elementary School and Parrsboro Regional High School serve the area for grades primary–12. The modern water treatment system uses drilled wells and a million-gallon reservoir that is a closed system providing high quality water. The sewage system does not include treatment and is discharged into Parrsboro Harbour.

Employment in Parrsboro is diversified with the largest employer being Parrsboro Metal Fabricators, located just outside town. There is substantial employment in the agriculture, forestry and fishing sectors, as well as in health, education and tourism.

As with most Nova Scotia towns, many young people leave Parrsboro for educational and employment opportunities, but some are returning to start new businesses or buy existing ones. Other new residents are being attracted to the security and quality of life available here, often starting second careers. Perhaps drawn by the affordable real estate, much of it built when shipping brought prosperity to Parrsboro, artists are also moving to the town and establishing galleries. This mix of new and old residents should enable Parrsboro to take advantage of its many strengths and regain the prosperity that it has enjoyed in the past.

Why 27th?

Parrsboro did very poorly in some categories, while doing extremely well in others. Placing 30th in both full-time earnings and family income is distressing. Salaries are obviously low regardless of the measurement method chosen. A 29th in employment rate is also cause for concern. Finally, a 28th in growth over 5 years and a 27th in growth over 40 years further brought down the overall rating.

On the positive side, a 3rd place in population density and a 5th place in land base are very important. A 7th place in early town status is a result of the town's prominent past, and an 8th in both affordable housing and climate for gardening also combined to improve the overall result. I should add that a 13th place in number of children is an indication of a balanced population that is a goal of many prominent towns.

Sources

www.town.parrsboro.ns.ca
www.shipscompany.com
http://museum.gov.ns.ca./fgm/

Clockwise from top: One of many historic homes, Town entrance sign, View from Ottawa House, Ottawa House, Ships Company Theatre sign, Glooscap statue.

Clockwise from top: Fort Anne National Historic Site, mural of Annapolis Royal in the past located in the downtown, historic home now Queen Anne Inn.

28

Annapolis Royal

Original Names

Mi'kmaq: Esunuskek (hard ground and well swarded)

French: Port Royal

English name: Annapolis Royal, in honour of Queen Anne, who ruled when the fort was captured for the last time in 1710

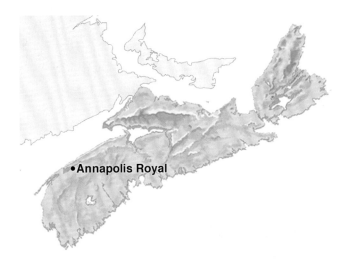

•Annapolis Royal

History

Settled first by Samuel de Champlain and Pierre Du Gua de Monts in 1605, this area comprises the oldest continuous European settlement north of St. Augustine, Florida. The area remained under French control for most of the seventeenth century, until the Treaty of Utrecht in 1713 granted it to the British for the last time.

Prior to the Treaty of Utrecht, the area was subject to frequent capture and, during this time, Fort Anne was begun in 1687 and completed in 1705. In 1690, the fort was attacked and the town burned by New England pirates. Occupied as a military post until 1854, it became a national park and museum in 1917.

In 1702 a building to be used as a hospital was built and furnished. Annapolis General Hospital was built in 1938-1939. A police force, no doubt the first in Nova Scotia, was organized by the council in 1734. In 1739, a school was built and a post office in 1785. In 1738, one of the first Masonic Lodges in Nova Scotia was organized.

The railway was started at Annapolis in 1867. Hugh Evan Gillis served as the first Mayor in 1893. The Annapolis District Community Centre was built by the Canadian Legion War Service during WW II, and incorporated as a community centre in 1946.

The economy has been based primarily on retail stores and as a shipping centre for the local fruit growing industry, as well as some fishing.

Annapolis Royal Today

Voted "the world's most liveable small town" (up to 20,000 population), by The International Awards for Liveable Communities in 2004, Nova Scotia's smallest town certainly is a delightful place. Home to some of North America's earliest European settlers, and historically a centre for the military and government, it is today popular with tourists due in part to this rich history and the architecture that has been lovingly preserved.

This is the Nova Scotia town most identified with arts and culture, as well as the environment. Many artists have moved to the area and visitors can enjoy a wide variety of locally produced crafts. Annapolis Royal is a very progressive town, evident in its recognition as one of five Cultural Capitals of Canada in 2005. It is home to the award-winning environmental group, Clean Annapolis River Project, and its use of a Ducks Unlimited wetland as part of its wastewater treatment system makes it a model for other small communities.

Annapolis Royal has a greater variety of services available than usual for such a small town. This is due to its status as a regional centre and its cooperative relationship with the neighbouring Municipality of Annapolis. Its unique sewage treatment system has made the town an environmental leader. The water treatment system draws from wells in Annapolis County and produces excellent water.

Attractions within the town include Fort Anne (Canada's oldest historic site), the Historic Gardens (ten acres of themed gardens), Kings Theatre, O'Dell House Museum, the many beautiful Bed and Breakfasts, as well as fine restaurants. The Annapolis Tidal Generating Station welcomes tourists. Built on an island within town limits, it is the only tidal power generating station in North America and produces one percent of Nova Scotia's electricity.

The town has a large retirement community and an excellent nursing home. However, to provide balance, the town needs to attract young families, especially those that will create home-based small businesses. Unfortunately, younger families have difficulty buying homes within the town as prices have risen dramatically. This problem cannot easily be solved by the town, as it not only has the smallest population, but also the smallest land base. Still, if any town can overcome this challenge, this is the one.

Why 28th?

Annapolis Royal is not accustomed to placing so poorly, but placements of last or next to last in 5 of the 14 categories had a dramatic effect on the overall placement. Placing 31st in both land base and affordable housing, and 30th in number of children, growth over 5 years and growth over 40 years, means that Annapolis Royal not only faces the problem of affordability, which is reducing the number of children within the town, but has suffered from a population reduction over several years.

On the positive side, placements of 1st in multicultural population (tied with Wolfville) and 1st in climate for gardening, as well as 7th in population density and 8th in university educated population were all helpful.

Sources

www.annapolisroyal.com
www.historicgardens.com

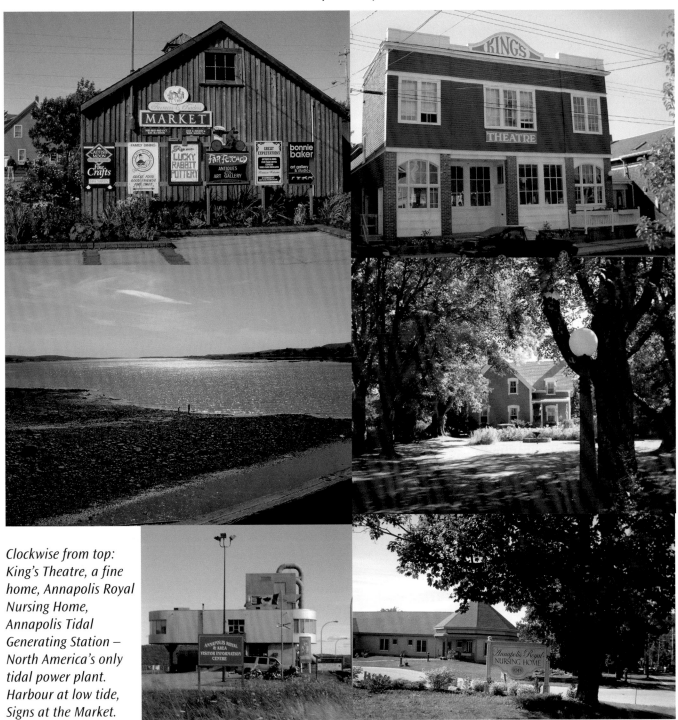

Clockwise from top: King's Theatre, a fine home, Annapolis Royal Nursing Home, Annapolis Tidal Generating Station – North America's only tidal power plant. Harbour at low tide, Signs at the Market.

Clockwise from top: Boardwalk on Water Street, Clam digging and Digby Town Hall.

29
Digby

Original Names

Mi'kmaq: Oositookun (an ear)
English: Digby. To honour Admiral Robert Digby, a previous name was changed in 1783, by Loyalists arriving in large numbers from New England in a convoy that he led

•**Digby**

History

English settlers from Brandywine in New England arrived in the area in 1766. Another group had moved from Annapolis in the same year. In 1783 the two groups were joined by large numbers of Loyalists arriving from New England and the settlement became known as Digby.

In 1784 a post office was opened in the home of Andrew Snodgrass, and James Foreman established a school in his home. The Anglican Trinity Church was consecrated in 1788.

The early town of Digby was fortified by a blockhouse on the hill and fortifications at the lower end of town. During the War of 1812, the inhabitants were frequently called out by real or false alarms of privateers and raiders from New England.

Regular ferry service to Saint John, New Brunswick, was begun with the *Sally* in 1784 and, in 1827, she was replaced by the *St. John*. The *Prince Rupert*, owned by the Dominion Atlantic Railway, replaced the *St. John* in 1895. These ships were followed by the *St. George* in 1913; the *Princess Helene* in 1930; and the *Princess of Acadia* in 1963. The last two were car ferries.

In the summer of 1891, the so-called missing link in the railway between Digby and Annapolis was completed, opening up direct Halifax-to-Yarmouth rail traffic. The cornerstone of the new courthouse was laid in 1909, and the new Digby Federal Building was opened in 1959. The Digby General Hospital was built in 1963-1965; and the Digby Pines Motor Hotel was built in 1928-1937, being sold to the province of Nova Scotia in 1965.

Digby Today

Digby is located on the Annapolis Basin of the Bay of Fundy, which gives its scallop fleet the best possible access to the fishing grounds. Its scallop fleet has earned Digby the title of "scallop capital of the world". Being on the Bay of Fundy, it also experiences the world's highest tides.

It is linked to the Valley towns by Kings Transit and, although closer to Yarmouth than to most Valley towns, it considers itself part of the Annapolis Valley. As it is also linked to Saint John, New Brunswick (across the Bay of Fundy) by Bay Ferries, Digby and Saint John have established a sister community relationship in which both communities work together to educate travelers as to what they each have to offer.

Although fishing is its best known and largest sector, Digby's employment is well diversified. Due to its natural beauty, many tourists have been attracted to the area and this has increased the number of jobs in tourism. As the regional centre for Digby County, the town has developed a strong retail and service sector. In addition, the regional schools and medical facilities provide educational and medical employment.

Two modern schools serve the town, Digby Elementary and Digby Regional High School. Both are located within the town, which enables students living in Digby to walk to school. The Nova Scotia Community College established a Digby campus in 2001 and Acadia University is available in Wolfville via Kings Transit.

The water is supplied to the town from deep water wells and requires only chlorination. The sewage treatment plant provides primary treatment and discharges into the Annapolis Basin. The town is also served by a library, arena, curling rink, community pool, museum, and marina. An 18-hole golf course is available at the nearby Pines Golf and Country Club, and the Admiral Digby Museum preserves the area's rich seafaring and cultural history.

Digby is the gateway to a spectacular natural region that is known for whale watching and seabird cruises. It celebrates its way of life and dependence on the sea with Digby Scallop Days, which take place every year during the second week of August. This special affinity with the sea is even noted in the architecture. Trinitiy Anglican Church, dating back to 1785, is the only church in Canada to have been built by shipwrights.

This is a very pleasant town, with no shortage of beaches and sunsets. In fact, Canadian Living Magazine judged that, in all of Canada, Digby is "the best place for romantics".

Why 29th

Digby had poor placements in over half of the categories and this resulted in a low overall placement. Of particular note is a 29th place for number of children, and 28th place in both full-time earnings and family income.

There were some positive results, including a 1st for climate for gardening, and a 7th for multicultural population.

Sources

www.townofdigby.ns.ca
www.bayferries.com
www.klis.com/digby/museum.html

Clockwise from top: Memorial Park, Impressive historic homes, Admiral Digby Museum, Art on wall of building, Digby Regional High School and Digby Pines with clam harvesters on beach.

Crescent Beach with town in distance, Locke family streetscape and Cape Island style boats in Lockeport Harbour.

30

Lockeport

Original Names

Mi'kmaq name: Sebunisk
English name: Lockeport, previously Ragged Island and Locke's Island, changed in 1870 to honour Jonathan Locke, an early resident

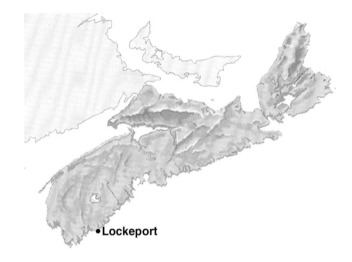

•Lockeport

History

Jonathan Locke, a native of Rhode Island, came to Liverpool in 1762. By 1767, he had joined with Joseph Hardy and Josiah Churchill to found the settlement that came to be known as Locke's Island. Located on a near-island in Ragged Islands Bay, it quickly developed a fishing industry.

During the 1770s, the local residents were so American in sympathy as to serve as advance bases for American privateers, but as the revolution wore on and their community, along with many other South Shore ports, suffered at the hands of these same American privateers, they turned against the revolutionary cause.

George Wadsworth taught school here in 1832, and a postal way office was established in 1846. A newspaper, the *Lockeport Hustler*, was begun in 1895. In the 1890s a strong West Indies trade flour-

ished, and blueberries were exported to the United States.

Churchill Locke served as the first Mayor in 1907. In the 20th century, Lockeport became known for its beaches, history, and hospitality, with tourism becoming a strong part of the economy.

Lockeport Today

Lockeport, described as "an island to sea", can rival Clark's Harbour with its spectacular location. The town sits on a near-island, connected to the mainland only by a narrow strip of land. Crescent Beach (which appeared on the back of the 1954 Canadian $50 bill), runs the length of this strip of land.

As might be expected, the major industry is

fishing, with Clearwater Fine Foods and R. Baker Fisheries being dominant employers. Allendale Electronics is also a major employer. As it is located only 15 minutes from the international shipping lanes, the town has drawn recreational yachting visitors from around the world. As a "full service" port, Lockeport services both recreational and commercial vessels up to 100 feet in length.

The provincial government supplies water to Lockeport's industries, but there is no town water system. A sewage treatment system has been in place since the late 1970s. The town has a range of services including a post office, bank, pharmacy, full service gas station, restaurants and bowling alley. Students within the town can walk to both Lockeport Elementary and Lockeport Regional High School.

The town has attracted tourists for many years and has continued to draw visitors and new residents. This is the perfect example of a town that is not visited unless it is a destination, as it is not located beside a busy highway. It is the ideal "get away".

There are certainly stresses in running a town with only 700 residents. In 2003, a town councillor was quoted by the Halifax Herald as calling for exploring amalgamation with nearby municipalities. The mayor at the time pointed out that many services, such as garbage collection, were already shared. This is a common way for towns to manage their resources effectively and most, including Lockeport, do work closely with neighboring municipalities.

Why 30th?

Lockport's population went from 1,200 in 1961 to 700 in 2001, which resulted in 31st place in the rating of population change during those years. This is in contrast to 5th place in population change from 1996-2001. It seems that the town is now reversing the population loss.

The results of most ratings were consistent with this placement, especially the university education rating, but there were several positive scores. Climate for gardening gained a 1st place as the nearby Gulf Stream moderates the temperatures, and the 3rd place in affordable housing is helpful. A 10th place in population density is a surprise, as it is a small land area, while 11th place in multicultural population points to the global popularity of Lockeport.

Source

www.geocities.com/lockeport_cap_webpage/townoflockeport

Opposite page: Clearwater fish plant, Crescent Beach.

Clockwise from top: Surf Lodge, Lockeport's Nursing Home; Spruce Street in Lockeport; Little School Museum; Icelandic monument; Col. Locke's Beach.

Clockwise from top: The three churches, Gazebo, Town Hall.

31

Mahone Bay

Original Names

Mi'kmaq: unknown, but the early name Mush-a-Mush probably had an Indian origin
French: La Baye de Toutes Iles (Bay of Many Islands)
English name: Mahone Bay, took over from Kinburn and thought to be derived from the French word mahonne, which refers to 'a particular type of low-slung pirate ship'

•Mahone Bay

History

A settlement was founded in 1754 by Captain Ephraim Cook, who established a mill here. Land was granted to Alexander and William Kedy around 1754. On June 27, 1813, a British warship cornered and destroyed the notorious pirate ship, the *Young Teaser*, in Mahone Bay. There are those that maintain that a phantom ship returns each year, on the anniversary of the event.

A school was established in 1820, with William Turner as master. The first St. James Anglican Church was dedicated in 1833, while a Methodist Church was erected in 1873, served as a town hall after 1925, and was torn down in 1952.

A postal way office was established in 1848 and a lighthouse was erected on Westhavers Island in 1894-95. Work was begun on the Mahone Bay – Halifax part of the South Shore Railway. *The*

Mahone Bay Signal was published from 1903-1908, and the *South Shore Record* began publication in 1932.

John McLean & Sons, Ltd., shipbuilders, began operating in 1861, incorporated in 1916, and sold and reorganized as the McLean Shipbuilding Co. in 1961. The Atlantic Bridge Company leased their premises in 1964.

Fishing, shipbuilding, tourism, trade and commerce have all been strong in the town's economy over the years.

Mahone Bay Today

Mahone Bay, known as "a treasure since 1754", is a picturesque town. The three churches, usually photographed from across the cove, have come to be representative of small town living. It is not surprising that tourism has become the major industry. R.P.S. Plastics, the Mahone Bay Nursing Home and the Bayview Community School also provide significant employment.

A sewage treatment plant was installed in 1994, and the first phase of a major upgrade of the water treatment system is currently underway. This will enable the town water system to meet new provincial environmental guidelines. Other infastructure improvements include a new elementary school, Bayview Community School, that was constructed in 2000.

The town of Mahone Bay is purchasing from the federal government the building that houses its post office. Advantages of this purchase include the retention of current parking spaces, a better position regarding Canada Post, as well as having space to lease.

The natural beauty and sense of community that has made the town an appealing place to live has driven up the price of housing with prices rising from $80,000 to $220,000 in a two year period and with many of the homes being sold to seasonal residents. The need for affordable housing is perhaps the biggest challenge facing Mahone Bay and this is currently before the town council. There are changes taking place: a new housing development, the first in 20 years, with 15-20 lots ranging in price from $40,000 to $60,000 is under construction. In addition, the Utilities and Review Board (URB) gave its approval to a 34-unit condominium complex, which will be located behind Suttles and Seawinds on Main Street.

Why 31st?

Mahone Bay's ranking came as quite a surprise. Unfortunately, the town had placements of 25th or worse in half of the 14 categories, and this was enough to give it last place. Receiving a 31st place in number of children meant that it had fewer children as a % of the population than any other town. The next worst category for Mahone Bay was a 30th for single population. This is a difficult category for most towns, as young people tend to move away for higher education or careers. Further compounding the negative results were a 29th place in affordable housing, a 28th place for early town status, a 27th place for land base, a 26th place for employment rate, and a 25th place for full-time earnings.

There were positive results. Mahone Bay placed 6th in both university educated population and multicultural population. A 9th place was received for family income and a 12th place for population density.

Sources

www.mahonebay.com
www.suttlesandseawinds.com
www.amospewter.com

Opposite page, clockwise from top: Mahone Bay Bed and Breakfast, Bayview Community School, Kedy's Landing sign, Mahone Bay from across the harbour, The Moorings Condominium, View from the water.

Town Rankings

A *area in square kilometres*. This category, also called land base, measures the land available for growth. This is a critical category for Antigonish, as shortage of land may lead to loss of town status.

B *date of incorporation*. This category, also called early town status, gives credit to the towns that were strong in the past and incorporated early.

C *average value of dwelling, in dollars*. This category, also called affordable housing, measures housing costs relative to other towns. The cost of housing often determines whether families can afford to live within a town, and I have therefore rewarded those that are most affordable.

D *average earnings for full-time employment*. This is a category that measures full-time earnings, but only traditional full-time employment is measured.

E *median family income*. This category includes non-traditional income that is not full-time. The two income categories give a balance so that no town is unfairly measured.

F *participation rate in the work force, as % of the population, 15 years of age and over*. This category is also called employment rate. A high employment rate is desireable and towns are rewarded accordingly.

G *plant hardiness zones*. This is the only category specifically for gardeners. It is also called climate for gardening and seemed a fairer measure than soil types. It did result in many tied scores as all Nova Scotia towns are located in one of four plant hardiness zones.

H *university certificate, diploma or degree recipients, as % of population*. This category is also abbreviated to university educated. Although this category favoured the university towns of Antigonish and Wolfville, as well as those located nearby, it was the only measure of educational attainment.

I *foreign born, as % of population, 15 years and over*. This category has been abbreviated to multicultural population. Although today multicultural often refers to visible minorities, I have included all foreign born and credited towns with the highest percentages as being the most cosmopolitan.

J *percentage of population under 15 years of age*. This category is also called number of children. All of the towns expressed a desire to attract young families, so towns that were most successful were rewarded with the highest scores.

K *population change 1996–2001*. This category is also called growth over 5 years.

L *population change 1961–2001*. This category is also called growth over 40 years.

M *population density per square kilometre*. Also called population density, this category does not give credit to the largest land base, but to the largest land base in relation to the smallest number of residents.

N *single as % of population, 15 years of age and over*. Also called single population, this is the only category for those seeking towns with other singles. Not a category for everyone, but it is important for balance.

	Area in square kilometres	
1	Truro	37.62
2	Mulgrave	17.81
3	Stewiacke	17.67
4	Kentville	17.35
5	Parrsboro	14.88
6	Westville	14.39
7	Bridgewater	13.61
8	Amherst	12.02
9	Springhill	11.15
10	Oxford	10.76
11	Yarmouth	10.56
12	New Glasgow	9.93
13	Windsor	9.06
14	Shelburne	9.00
15	Stellarton	8.99
16	Port Hawkesbury	8.35
17	Pictou	7.94
18	Berwick	6.80
19	Wolfville	6.45
20	Trenton	6.01
21	Middleton	5.44
22	Canso	5.40
23	Antigonish	5.15
24	Lunenburg	4.01
25	Bridgetown	3.54
26	Digby	3.15
27	Mahone Bay	3.13
28	Clark's Harbour	2.90
29	Lockeport	2.32
30	Hantsport	2.13
31	Annapolis Royal	2.05

Source: Service Nova Scotia and Municipal Relations, Annual Report, 2004

	Ranking of incorporated towns by date of incorporation	
1	Pictou	1874
2	New Glasgow	1875
2	Truro	1875
4	Windsor	1878
5	Kentville	1886
6	Lunenburg	1888
7	Amherst	1889
7	Antigonish	1889
7	Parrsboro	1889
7	Port Hawkesbury	1889
7	Springhill	1889
7	Stellarton	1889
13	Digby	1890
13	Yarmouth	1890
15	Annapolis Royal	1892
16	Wolfville	1893
17	Westville	1894
18	Hantsport	1895
19	Bridgetown	1897
20	Bridgewater	1899
21	Canso	1901
22	Oxford	1904
23	Stewiacke	1906
24	Lockeport	1907
24	Shelburne	1907
26	Middleton	1909
27	Trenton	1911
28	Clark's Harbour	1919
28	Mahone Bay	1919
30	Berwick	1923
30	Mulgrave	1923

Source: Service Nova Scotia and Municipal Relations, Annual Report, 2004

	Average value of dwelling in dollars (Nova Scotia average 101515)	
1	Canso	42,936
2	Springhill	53,181
3	Lockeport	55,022
4	Trenton	60,726
5	Westville	61,421
6	Pictou	62,595
7	Mulgrave	62,663
8	Parrsboro	69,715
9	Oxford	72,797
10	Stellarton	75,108
11	Shelburne	75,531
12	Bridgetown	78,488
13	Amherst	78,865
14	Digby	84,384
15	Clark's Harbour	84,689
16	Middleton	85,738
17	New Glasgow	87,188
18	Yarmouth	88,531
19	Port Hawkesbury	91,716
20	Stewiacke	93,806
21	Truro	96,126
22	Hantsport	96,259
23	Berwick	99,130
24	Windsor	99,895
25	Bridgewater	100,505
26	Kentville	110,242
27	Antigonish	114,595
28	Lunenburg	125,548
29	Mahone Bay	143,821
30	Wolfville	163,569
31	Annapolis Royal	164,556

Source: Based on Statistics Canada Census 2001 Community Profiles

	Average earnings for full time employment (Nova Scotia average 37,872)	
1	Lunenburg	50,664
2	New Glasgow	43,901
3	Wolfville	43,583
4	Port Hawkesbury	40,002
5	Antigonish	39,534
6	Pictou	39,514
7	Berwick	39,010
8	Stellarton	37,133
9	Stewiacke	37,106
10	Kentville	37,034
11	Mulgrave	36,128
12	Shelburne	35,464
13	Annapolis Royal	35,345
14	Bridgewater	34,940
15	Hantsport	34,382
16	Westville	34,095
17	Windsor	33,597
18	Middleton	33,418
19	Truro	33,250
20	Springhill	33,184
21	Bridgetown	32,869
22	Yarmouth	32,804
23	Trenton	31,808
24	Amherst	30,718
25	Mahone Bay	30,376
26	Oxford	30,048
27	Lockeport	29,061
28	Digby	27,751
29	Canso	27,098
30	Parrsboro	26,104
31	Clark's Harbour	23,454

Source: Based on Statistics Canada Census 2001 Community Profiles

	Median family income–all census families (Nova Scotia average 46,523)	
1	Wolfville	57,028
2	Antigonish	53,628
3	Port Hawkesbury	50,935
4	Kentville	49,854
5	Clark's Harbour	47,995
6	Hantsport	47,585
7	New Glasgow	46,595
8	Pictou	46,302
9	Mahone Bay	45,027
10	Stellarton	44,737
11	Berwick	44,272
12	Bridgewater	44,228
13	Lunenburg	42,549
14	Middleton	42,493
15	Canso	42,321
16	Bridgetown	42,302
17	Oxford	41,677
18	Shelburne	41,535
19	Stewiacke	41,343
20	Annapolis Royal	40,949
21	Windsor	40,685
22	Truro	40,632
23	Trenton	40,529
24	Westville	40,391
25	Springhill	40,366
26	Amherst	38,831
27	Mulgrave	38,592
28	Digby	38,541
29	Lockeport	36,482
30	Parrsboro	33,208
31	Yarmouth	30,514

Source: Based on Statistics Canada Census 2001 Community Profiles

	Participation rate in the work force as % of the population 15 years of age and over (Nova Scotia average 61.6)	
1	Shelburne	64.6
2	Clark's Harbour	64.5
3	Mulgrave	63.9
4	Port Hawkesbury	62.9
5	Amherst	61.2
6	Canso	60.5
7	Pictou	60.2
8	Oxford	60.1
9	Kentville	60.0
10	Wolfville	59.9
11	Bridgewater	59.7
12	Berwick	59.4
13	Hantsport	59.0
14	Windsor	58.2
15	Trenton	58.0
16	Stellarton	57.4
17	Antigonish	57.3
18	New Glasgow	57.1
18	Truro	57.1
20	Annapolis Royal	56.7
21	Lunenburg	56.1
22	Stewiacke	55.7
23	Westville	55.5
24	Yarmouth	55.3
25	Digby	54.9
26	Mahone Bay	54.2
27	Bridgetown	52.3
28	Lockeport	50.9
29	Parrsboro	50.8
30	Springhill	46.5
31	Middleton	44.4

Source: Based on Statistics Canada Census 2001 Community Profiles

	Plant hardiness zones	
1	Annapolis Royal	6a
1	Clark's Harbour	6a
1	Digby	6a
1	Lockeport	6a
1	Lunenburg	6a
1	Shelburne	6a
1	Yarmouth	6a
8	Amherst	5a
8	Antigonish	5a
8	Mulgrave	5a
8	New Glasgow	5a
8	Parrsboro	5a
8	Pictou	5a
8	Springhill	5a
8	Stellarton	5a
8	Trenton	5a
8	Truro	5a
8	Westville	5a
19	Berwick	5b
19	Bridgetown	5b
19	Bridgewater	5b
19	Canso	5b
19	Hantsport	5b
19	Kentville	5b
19	Mahone Bay	5b
19	Middleton	5b
19	Oxford	5b
19	Port Hawkesbury	5b
19	Stewiacke	5b
19	Windsor	5b
19	Wolfville	5b

Source: Agriculture and Agri-food Canada

	University certificate, diploma or degree recipients as % of population	
1	Wolfville	51.1
2	Antigonish	37.7
3	Kentville	27.6
4	Lunenburg	24.8
5	Truro	24.6
6	Mahone Bay	24.0
7	Hantsport	22.2
8	Annapolis Royal	21.7
8	Berwick	21.7
10	New Glasgow	20.4
11	Windsor	19.0
12	Bridgewater	18.2
13	Pictou	15.8
14	Port Hawkesbury	15.2
14	Stellarton	15.2
16	Oxford	14.2
17	Bridgetown	14.0
18	Yarmouth	13.8
19	Amherst	13.4
20	Middleton	13.3
20	Shelburne	13.3
22	Canso	13.2
23	Digby	9.2
24	Parrsboro	9.1
25	Stewiacke	8.9
26	Springhill	8.6
27	Westville	7.6
28	Trenton	6.5
29	Clark's Harbour	4.6
29	Mulgrave	4.6
31	Lockeport	3.9

Source: Based on Statistics Canada Census 2001 Community Profiles

	Foreign born as % of population 15 years and over	
1	Annapolis Royal	12
1	Wolfville	12
3	Bridgetown	9
4	Middleton	8
5	Antigonish	7
6	Mahone Bay	6
7	Bridgewater	5
7	Digby	5
7	Kentville	5
7	Lunenburg	5
11	Hantsport	4
11	Lockeport	4
11	New Glasgow	4
11	Shelburne	4
11	Stewiacke	4
11	Truro	4
11	Windsor	4
18	Berwick	3
18	Clark's Harbour	3
18	Pictou	3
18	Yarmouth	3
22	Amherst	2
22	Oxford	2
22	Parrsboro	2
22	Port Hawkesbury	2
22	Stellarton	2
22	Trenton	2
22	Westville	2
29	Mulgrave	1
29	Springhill	1
31	Canso	0

Source: Based on Statistics Canada Census 2001 Community Profiles

	% of population under 15 years of age (Nova Scotia average 18.2)	
1	Stewiacke	22.7
2	Westville	20.5
3	Mulgrave	20.4
4	Port Hawkesbury	19.9
5	Clark's Harbour	19
6	Yarmouth	18.7
7	Stellarton	18.6
8	Hantsport	18.3
9	Trenton	18.1
10	Berwick	17.9
11	Pictou	17.8
12	Oxford	17.7
13	Parrsboro	17.6
14	Amherst	17.3
15	Shelburne	17.1
16	Middleton	17
17	Bridgetown	16.9
18	Windsor	16.8
19	Antigonish	16.5
20	Kentville	16.3
20	New Glasgow	16.3
22	Springhill	16.1
23	Bridgewater	15.9
24	Lockeport	15.7
25	Canso	15.6
26	Truro	14.9
27	Lunenburg	14.4
27	Wolfville	14.4
29	Digby	13.7
30	Annapolis Royal	13.5
31	Mahone Bay	12.6

Source: Based on Statistics Canada Census 2001 Community Profiles

	Population change 1996 - 2001			
		1996	2001	Change
1	Bridgetown	994	1035	4.1
2	Berwick	2195	2282	4.0
3	Bridgewater	7351	7621	3.7
4	Windsor	3726	3778	1.4
5	Lockeport	692	701	1.3
6	Kentville	5551	5610	1.1
7	Mulgrave	896	904	0.9
8	Yarmouth	7568	7561	-0.1
9	Lunenburg	2599	2568	-1.2
9	Stewiacke	1405	1388	-1.2
11	Oxford	1352	1332	-1.5
12	Amherst	9669	9470	-2.1
13	Antigonish	4860	4754	-2.2
14	Springhill	4193	4091	-2.4
14	Westville	3976	3879	-2.4
16	Mahone Bay	1017	991	-2.6
17	Port Hawkesbury	3809	3701	-2.8
18	Middleton	1800	1744	-3.1
19	Stellarton	4968	4809	-3.2
20	Pictou	4022	3875	-3.7
20	Clark's Harbour	980	944	-3.7
22	New Glasgow	9812	9432	-3.9
23	Truro	11938	11457	-4.0
23	Digby	2199	2111	-4.0
23	Hantsport	1252	1202	-4.0
26	Wolfville	3833	3658	-4.6
27	Trenton	2952	2798	-5.2
28	Parrsboro	1617	1529	-5.4
29	Shelburne	2132	2013	-5.6
30	Annapolis Royal	583	550	-5.7
31	Canso	1127	992	-12.0

Source: Based on Statistics Canada Census 2001 Community Profiles

| | Population change 1961 - 2001 | | | |

		1961	2001	Change
1	Port Hawkesbury	1346	3701	174.9
2	Berwick	1282	2282	78.0
3	Bridgewater	4497	7621	69.4
4	Wolfville	2413	3658	51.5
5	Stewiacke	1042	1388	33.2
6	Kentville	4612	5610	21.6
7	Antigonish	4344	4754	9.4
8	Clark's Harbour	945	944	.1
9	Bridgetown	1043	1035	-.7
10	Windsor	3823	3778	-1.1
11	New Glasgow	9782	9432	-3.5
12	Westville	4159	3879	-6.7
13	Truro	12421	11457	-7.7
14	Digby	2308	2111	-8.5
15	Middleton	1921	1744	-9.2
16	Oxford	1471	1332	-9.4
17	Stellarton	5327	4809	-9.7
18	Mahone Bay	1103	991	-10.1
19	Trenton	3140	2798	-10.8
20	Amherst	10788	9470	-12.2
21	Yarmouth	8636	7561	-12.4
22	Hantsport	1381	1202	-12.9
23	Canso	1151	992	-13.8
24	Pictou	4534	3875	-14.5
25	Lunenburg	3056	2568	-15.9
26	Shelburne	2408	2013	-16.4
27	Parrsboro	1834	1529	-16.6
28	Mulgrave	1145	904	-21.0
29	Springhill	5836	4091	-29.9
30	Annapolis Royal	800	550	-31.2
31	Lockeport	1231	701	-43.0

Source: Based on Statistics Canada Census 2001 Community Profiles

	Population density per square kilometre	
1	Mulgrave	50.8
2	Stewiacke	78.6
3	Parrsboro	102.7
4	Oxford	123.8
5	Canso	183.6
6	Shelburne	223.6
7	Annapolis Royal	268.0
8	Westville	269.6
9	Bridgetown	292.1
10	Lockeport	302.1
11	Truro	304.5
12	Mahone Bay	316.7
13	Middleton	320.7
14	Kentville	323.3
15	Clark's Harbour	325.4
16	Berwick	335.5
17	Springhill	366.8
18	Windsor	417.0
19	Port Hawkesbury	443.5
20	Trenton	465.9
21	Pictou	488.0
22	Stellarton	534.8
23	Bridgewater	560.1
24	Hantsport	564.9
25	Wolfville	567.0
26	Lunenburg	640.5
27	Digby	670.8
28	Yarmouth	716.1
29	Amherst	787.9
30	Antigonish	923.9
31	New Glasgow	950.2

Source: Based on Statistics Canada Census 2001 Community Profiles

	Single as % of population – 15 years of age and over	
1	Antigonish	49
2	Wolfville	36
3	Port Hawkesbury	35
4	Yarmouth	34
5	Canso	33
5	Truro	33
7	Kentville	32
7	Shelburne	32
7	Windsor	32
10	Mulgrave	31
10	New Glasgow	31
10	Springhill	31
10	Trenton	31
10	Westville	31
15	Amherst	30
15	Pictou	30
15	Stellarton	30
18	Clark's Harbour	29
18	Digby	29
20	Bridgewater	28
21	Middleton	26
22	Annapolis Royal	25
22	Parrsboro	25
24	Berwick	24
24	Lockeport	24
24	Lunenburg	24
24	Oxford	24
24	Stewiacke	24
29	Bridgetown	23
30	Mahone Bay	22
31	Hantsport	20

Source: Based on Statistics Canada Census 2001 Community Profiles